VIETNAM

GOOD STORIES REVEAL as much, or more, about a locale as any map or guidebook. Whereabouts Press is dedicated to publishing books that will enlighten a traveler to the soul of a place. By bringing a country's stories to the English-speaking reader, we hope to convey its culture through literature. Books from Whereabouts Press are essential companions for the curious traveler, and for the person who appreciates how fine writing enhances one's experiences in the world.

"Coming newly into Spanish, I lacked two essentials—a childhood in the language, which I could never acquire, and a sense of its literature, which I could."

—Alastair Reid, *Whereabouts: Notes on Being a Foreigner*

OTHER TRAVELER'S LITERARY COMPANIONS

Amsterdam edited by Manfred Wolf

Australia edited by Robert Ross

Chile edited by Katherine Silver

Costa Rica edited by Barbara Ras
with a foreword by Oscar Arias

Cuba edited by Ann Louise Bardach

Greece edited by Artemis Leontis

Israel edited by Michael Gluzman and Naomi Seidman
with a foreword by Robert Alter

Italy edited by and translated by Lawrence Venuti

Mexico edited by C. M. Mayo

Prague edited by Paul Wilson

Spain edited by Peter Bush and Lisa Dillman

VIETNAM

A TRAVELER'S LITERARY COMPANION

EDITED BY

JOHN BALABAN
AND
NGUYEN QUI DUC

WHEREABOUTS PRESS
BERKELEY, CALIFORNIA

Copyright © 1996 by Whereabouts Press
(complete copyright information on page 238)

Published in the United States by
Whereabouts Press
www.whereaboutspress.com

Distributed to the trade by
Consortium Book Sales & Distribution

Map of Vietnam by Bill Nelson

Manufactured in the United States of America
on recycled paper.

Library of Congress Cataloging-in-Publication Data

Vietnam : a traveler's literary companion /
edited by John Balaban and Nguyen Qui Duc.
p.   cm.—(Traveler's literary companions)
Short stories translated from Vietnamese.
ISBN 1-883513-02-2 (alk. paper)
I. Balaban, John, 1943– . II. Nguyen, Qui Duc. III. Series.
PL4378.82.E5V54   1996
895'.92230108—dc20   95-46930
CIP

5   4   3

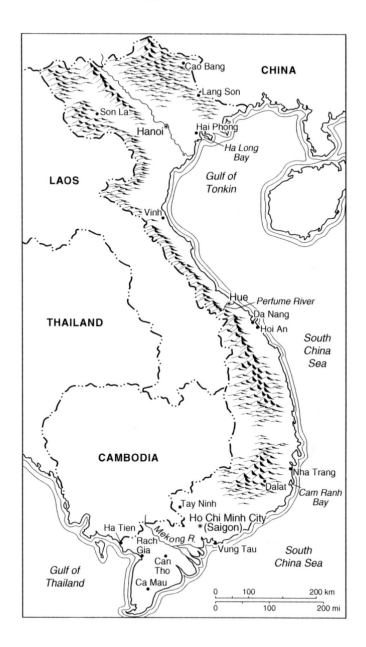

Contents

DALAT

VILLAGES

REMEMBRANCE

Preface

The literary traveler to Vietnam is in for pleasant surprises. Reading these stories will be like seeing Vietnam for the first time, hearing Vietnamese speaking to themselves of their deepest concerns and pleasures, beyond the disfigurements of the last war, beyond its snapshots and captions and journalistic interpreters. All our stories come from the best Vietnamese writers, at home and abroad. Their stories are set within the microcosms of peasant society, in the floating world of Saigon's commercialism, within the hierarchies of Marxist privilege, and in the bittersweet memories of an old man stalled at a traffic light in southern California.

Hanoi. The mysterious mountain jungles. The demimondes of the Hue court and the Saigon cafés. A rural commune. A raucous tailor shop. Just as they traverse wide landscapes, these stories also harken through time to the roots of Vietnamese society. Nguyen Du, an early nineteenth-century mandarin, figures in one story; a phrase from the 2000-year-old *Heart Sutra* closes another. Western readers — prepared to see Vietnam in modern terms — will often find themselves drawn instead into the ancient habits of the "Three Religions," the

Taoism, Buddhism, and Confucianism that laid claim to Vietnamese thinking long before the West arrived.

We have avoided war stories. The Vietnamese condition is too large and complex to see it solely through the dark lens of the recent war, although inevitably the war echoes in some of the tales told here and many of the country's best writers, like Bao Ninh and Duong Thu Huong, suffered in the war and survived to write about it.

We have also tried to avoid politics or, less naively, we have avoided stories carrying heavy political freight. We sought works from as wide a range of authors as we could summon. They come from the North and from the South. Some are now refugees in America. One of our authors is a Buddhist monk; another, a restaurateur. Our primary concern in collecting these stories was quality.

We are aware that we missed important writers such as Le Luu and Vo Phien, Tran Van Dinh, Mai Thao, Le Tat Dieu, Tran Da Tu, Nha Ca, and Mai Kim Ngoc. We were looking for stories redolent with place and culture.

Another issue affects the familiarity, if not the quality, of the fiction here: While Vietnamese have been telling stories about themselves for 2000 years—writing first in Chinese, then in Vietnamese *nom*, and finally in the current roman alphabet—almost all of that literary expression has been through poetry. A good deal of that traditional poetry is *oral*, committed to popular memory, rarely written down, as in the *ca dao* lyric poems or the *vong co* tales of warriors and princesses still chanted by blind singers at ferry crossings and in public parks. Often, Vietnamese would take Chinese prose novels and translate them into poetic adaptations, most notably Nguyen Du's *Tale of Kieu.*

Thus the Western-style short story and novel are fairly recent acquisitions.* The first novel, Tran Chanh Chieu's *The Unjust Suffering of Hoang To Anh*, dates from 1910; the first short story, Nguyen Trong Quan's "The Story of Lazaro Phien," from 1887. Correspondingly, the influences on Vietnamese prose fiction are quite different from ours: the ancient oral folk poetries, the poeticized Chinese novels of the "knight-errant" and "scholar-beauty" types, eighteenth- and nineteenth-century French novels of romantic adventure and naturalism (particularly Rousseau, Chateaubriand, Lamartine, Hugo, Zola, and Dumas, *père*), and, most recently, Soviet social realism.

So not only these tales, but their telling will be of interest to the literary traveler. Some will seem quite simple, like Doan Quoc Sy's elaboration on a folk poem at least one hundred years old. Another—Nguyen Huy Thiep's "Fired Gold"—may seem positively Borgesian although Mr. Thiep, who is arguably Vietnam's pre-eminent literary craftsman, most likely has never encountered the complex Argentine.

When farmers have to leave the small, intense world of their village and journey out into the wider world, they are comforted by all sorts of proverbial advice. One proverb comes to mind as a final word to the literary traveler to Vietnam: *Di mot ngay dang, hoc mot sang khon.* "Go out today, and return with a basket full of wisdom."

—John Balaban and Nguyen Qui Duc

*For a detailed discussion, see John C. Schafer and The Uyen, "The Novel Emerges in Cochinchina," *The Journal of Asian Studies* 52, no. 4 (November 1993): 854–884.

Salt of the Jungle

Nguyen Huy Thiep

A MONTH after the new year is the best time to be in the jungle. The vegetation is bursting with fresh buds, and its leaves are deep green and moist. Nature is both daunting and delicate, and this is due, in large measure, to the showers of spring rain.

At around this time, your feet sink into carpets of rotting leaves, you inhale pure air, and, sometimes, your body shudders with pleasure, because a drop of water has fallen from a leaf and struck your bare shoulder. Miraculously, the vexations of your daily life can be completely forgotten, because a small squirrel has sprung onto a branch. And, as it happened, it was at just such a time that Mr. Dieu went hunting.

The idea to go hunting had come to him when his son, who was studying in a foreign country, sent him a gift of a double-barreled shotgun. The gun was as light as a toy, and so sleek that he could not have dreamt such a beautiful thing existed. Mr. Dieu was sixty, and, at that age, both a new shotgun and a spring day for the hunt really made life worth living.

To dress for the occasion, he put on a warm quilted coat and trousers, a fur hat, and laced up a pair of high boots.

To be well prepared, he also took a ration of sticky rice rolled into a ball the size of his fist. He moved up along the bed of a dry stream toward its source, a mile from which was the fabled kingdom of limestone caves.

Mr. Dieu turned onto a beaten track that wound through the jungle. As he moved along, he was aware that the trees on either side were full of bluebirds. Yet, he did not shoot. With a gun like his, it would have been a waste of ammunition, especially when he had already had his fill of bluebirds. They were tasty enough, but had a fishy flavor. In any case, he had no need to shoot birds with a loft full of pigeons at home.

At a turn in the track, Mr. Dieu was startled by a rustling in a bush. A clump of motley vines flew up in front of his face, and, as he caught his breath, a pair of jungle fowls shot out in front of the bush with their heads down, clucking. Mr. Dieu raised his shotgun and aimed. However, the fowls did not present a good target. *I'll miss*, he thought. He considered the situation, and sat down motionless for a very long time, waiting for the jungle to become quiet again. The fowls would think there was nobody there: it would be better that way—for them and for him.

The mountain range was full of towering peaks. Mr. Dieu looked at them as he contemplated his strength. To bag a monkey or a mountain goat would certainly be something. But he knew that mountain goats were difficult game. It was only by some stroke of luck that he would get a good shot at one, and he did not think that luck would come.

As he weighed carefully the pros and cons, Mr. Dieu decided to move along the foot of the limestone mountain range and hunt monkeys in the Dau Da Forest. He would be surer of finding food and wasting less energy. Mount Hoa Qua and Thuy Liem Cave were along the valley and, like the forest, they were legendary monkey haunts. Mr. Dieu also knew that he did not have difficulty shooting monkeys.

He stopped on a piece of rising ground, amid trees covered with climbing vines. This species of tree was unknown to him, with its silver leaves and golden flowers like earrings that hung down to the earth. Mr. Dieu sat quietly and observed, for he wanted to see if there were any monkeys there. These animals are as crafty as human beings; when they gather food they always put out sentries, and monkey sentries are very acute. If you don't see them, there is no hope for the hunt, no hope of hitting the leader of the troop. Of course, the leader was only a monkey. But it was not just any monkey. It would be the one that fate had singled out for him. So he had to wait, had to be cunning if he wanted to shoot his monkey.

Mr. Dieu sat quietly and relaxed for half an hour. The spring weather was warm and silky. It had been a long time since he had had the opportunity to sit as peacefully as this. And as he sat without a care in the world, the tranquillity of the jungle flowed through his being.

Suddenly, a swishing sound came rushing from out of the Dau Da Forest. It was the sound of a large animal moving through the trees. Mr. Dieu knew it was the leader of a monkey troop. He also knew that this monkey was formidable. It would appear with the brutal self-confidence of a king. Mr. Dieu smiled and watched carefully.

The sound continued for a while; then, suddenly, the

beast appeared. It rapidly propelled itself through the jungle as though it never rested. Mr. Dieu admired its nimbleness. However, it disappeared in a flash, leaving him with a sharp stab of disappointment that this king-like creature would not be his. The elation he had felt since leaving home that morning was beginning to subside.

As soon as the leader disappeared, a gaggle of about twenty monkeys swung into view, criss-crossing Mr. Dieu's field of vision from very many angles. Some of them appeared on perches high up in the trees, others swung through the branches, and still others sprang to the ground. Within this medley of movement, Mr. Dieu noticed three monkeys that stayed together: a male, a female, and their young baby. He knew immediately that this male monkey was his prey.

Mr. Dieu felt hot. He took off his hat and quilted coat and placed them under a bush. He also placed his ball of sticky rice there. Gradually, he moved into a depression in the ground. He observed carefully, and noticed that the female monkey was standing guard. That was convenient, for with a becoming sense of vanity, she had distracted herself with the task of picking off her body lice.

Mr. Dieu made his calculations, then crept along, keeping windward of the female monkey. He had to get within twenty meters of the troop before he would be able to shoot. He crawled rapidly and skillfully. Once he had located his prey, he was sure he would kill it. That monkey was his. He was so certain of this, he felt that if he stumbled or made a careless move it would not make any difference.

Yet, even though he thought like this, Mr. Dieu still stalked the monkey troop carefully. He knew that nature was full of surprises, that one could never be too cautious.

He rested the shotgun in the fork of a tree, while the family trio had no inkling that disaster was near. The father was perched in a tree plucking fruit and throwing it down to the mother and child. Before he threw it, he always selected the best fruit and ate it himself. *How contemptible,* thought Mr. Dieu as he squeezed the trigger. The shotgun blast stunned the monkey troop for several seconds: the male monkey had fallen heavily to the ground with its arms outstretched.

The confusion into which the shotgun blast had thrown the monkey troop caused Mr. Dieu to tremble. He had done something cruel. His arms and legs went limp, with the kind of sensation that overcomes someone who has just overexerted himself with heavy work, and the troop disappeared into the jungle before he knew it. The female monkey and the baby also ran off after the others, but, after moving some distance, the female suddenly turned around and returned. Her mate, whose shoulder had been shattered by the shotgun pellets, was trying to raise himself but kept falling back to the ground.

The female monkey advanced carefully to where her mate had fallen and looked around, suspicious of the silence. The male monkey let out a pitiful scream, before he became silent again and listened, with a frantic expression on his face.

Oh, get away from there! Mr. Dieu groaned softly. But the female monkey looked as though she was prepared to sacrifice herself. She went to her mate and lifted him up in her arms. Mr. Dieu angrily raised his shotgun. Her readiness to sacrifice herself made him hate her like some bourgeois madame who paraded her noble nature. He knew all about the deceptions in which such theatrical performances were rooted; she could not deceive an old hunter like him.

As Mr. Dieu prepared to squeeze the trigger, the female monkey turned around and looked at him with terror in her eyes. She dropped the male monkey with a thud and fled. Mr. Dieu breathed a sigh of relief, then laughed quietly. He rose to his feet and left his hiding place.

I've made a mistake! Mr. Dieu cursed under his breath. For when he moved from his hiding place, the female monkey immediately turned around. *She knows I'm human,* he sighed, *the game is up.* Exactly so: the female monkey now kept him in the corner of her eye as she rushed headlong back to her mate. She deftly put her arms around him and hugged him to her chest. The two rolled around in a ball on the ground. She was acting like a crazy old woman. She was going to sacrifice herself recklessly, because of some noble instinct that nature prized. This stirred deep feelings of guilt in Mr. Dieu's heart. He had revealed himself as an assassin, while the female monkey, who faced death, still bared her teeth in a smile. Whatever he did now, he could only suffer, he could never rest, and he could even die two years before his time if he shot the female monkey at this moment. And all of this was because he had come out of his hiding place two minutes too soon.

As if to torment him, the monkeys took each other by

the hand and ran off. *You pathetic old figure, Dieu,* he thought sadly. *With a pair of arthritic legs like yours, how are you going to run as fast as a monkey driven by loyalty and devotion?* The female monkey waved her bow legs, grinned, and made obscene gestures. Mr. Dieu angrily hurled his shotgun down in front of him. He wanted to frighten the female monkey into releasing her mate.

At the moment the shotgun hit the ground, the baby monkey suddenly appeared from a rocky mound. It grabbed the sling of the shotgun and dragged it off along the ground. The three monkeys scurried off on all fours, shrieking. Mr. Dieu was struck dumb for a second, then burst out laughing: his predicament was so ridiculous.

He picked up a handful of dirt and stones and threw it at the monkeys, as he took off howling in pursuit. The monkeys, who were terrified by these developments, split up, with the two adults veering off in the direction of the mountains and the baby running toward the cliff. *Losing the shotgun will be disastrous,* thought Mr. Dieu, and he continued to chase the baby monkey. He charged forward and narrowed the distance between them to the extent that only a jagged rock prevented him from reaching his gun.

By chasing the baby monkey, Mr. Dieu had taken a course of action that had extraordinary consequences. These began when the small monkey just rolled over the edge of the precipice, holding the shotgun sling tightly. Evidently, it was too inexperienced to react in any other way.

Mr. Dieu was pale and soaked with sweat. He stood looking down over the cliff with his body shaking. From

far below came the echo of a piercing scream, the likes of
which he had never heard before. He drew back in fear, as
a mist swirled up from the abyss and enveloped the vegetation around him. Very quickly the entire landscape was
obscured by eerie vapors. He ran back to the mountain. It
was perhaps the first time since childhood that Mr. Dieu
had run as though he were being chased by a ghost.

Mr. Dieu was exhausted when he reached the foot of
the mountain. He sat down on the ground, looking back
in the direction of the precipice, which the mist had now
obscured. He remembered suddenly that this was the
most feared place in the valley: the place that hunters
called Death Hollow. Here, with alarming regularity,
somebody perished in the mist each year.

Ghosts? thought Mr. Dieu. *Forsaken spirits usually take
the form of white monkeys, don't they?* It had been a white
monkey that seized the gun. Moreover, this had been
such an extraordinary action that Mr. Dieu began to
wonder if what he had been chasing was really a monkey.

Am I dreaming? he wondered, looking around. *Is all of
this happening?* He stood up and looked at the mountain
wall on the other side of Death Hollow. He was stunned,
for now, without a trace of mist, the dome of the sky was
clear and vast, and the entire landscape was visible in
every detail.

An agitated cry came from somewhere above him. Mr.
Dieu looked up and there he saw the wounded monkey
lying across a rock ledge. The female monkey was nowhere to be seen, and so, very happy in the certainty that
he would now catch his monkey, Mr. Dieu searched for a
way to climb up on the rock ledge.

Finding a way up the side of the steep, slippery mountain was both difficult and dangerous. Mr. Dieu gauged his strength. *Whatever way, I'm going to get that monkey,* he murmured to himself, as he calmly used the crevices in the rock face to work his way up.

After about ten minutes, Mr. Dieu felt hot. He chose a spot where he could stand, then took off his boots and outer garments and placed them in the fork of a mulberry tree. He climbed onward quickly with no doubts about his ability to reach the ledge.

The slab of rock on which the wounded monkey lay was smooth and seemed somewhat unstable. Beneath it, there was a crevice as wide as Mr. Dieu's hand, which would allow him to pull himself up. He shuddered, frightened by the feeling that the slab might move and roll down the mountain at any moment. Nature was cruel and might want to test his courage further.

Mr. Dieu finally pulled himself up on the rock ledge with his elbows, and there he saw an extremely beautiful monkey with fine golden hair. It lay prone with its hands raking across the surface of the rock, as if it were trying to pull itself along. Its shoulder was stained red with blood.

Mr. Dieu put his hand on the monkey and felt its feverish body heat. *Easier than putting a hand on a sparrow,* he thought. Next, he slipped his hand under the monkey's chest and lifted it to estimate its weight. However, he withdrew his hand quickly when the chest emitted a low, but very disconcerting *hum,* which made him feel that his intervention had aroused Death's fury. The monkey stirred Mr. Dieu's pity when it trembled and rolled its sluggish eyes toward him. The shotgun pellets had smashed the monkey's shoulder blade and come out through four centimeters of bone. Each time the bones rubbed together, the monkey writhed in pain.

"I can't leave you like that," said Mr. Dieu. He picked up some Lao grass, crumpled it in his hand, and put it in the monkey's mouth. The monkey chewed the grass carefully, while Mr. Dieu applied a handful of leaves to its wound to stem the bleeding. The monkey curled its body into a ball and again turned its moist eyes toward Mr. Dieu. The old man looked away.

The monkey then buried its head in Mr. Dieu's arms, and a stammering sound came out of its mouth. The monkey was like a helpless child imploring him for help. Mr. Dieu felt very miserable. "It is better for me if you resist," he murmured, looking down at the suffering brow of the shriveled monkey. "I am old, and you know the sympathy of old people is easily aroused. What can I use to bandage you, poor monkey?"

Mr. Dieu considered the situation. He had no choice but to take off his shorts and use them to bandage the monkey's wound. When he did this, the bleeding stopped and the monkey no longer groaned.

Naked now, Mr. Dieu picked the monkey up and kept adjusting its weight in his arms as he found his way back down the mountain. Then, suddenly, as though impelled by some force, the mountainside began to slide away with a tremendous roar from about halfway up.

An avalanche!

Mr. Dieu jumped in terror and clung tightly to a rock. A section of the path he had taken to come up the mountain now flashed down past him, leaving only the surface of the rock shorn smooth. Mr. Dieu could no longer see the mulberry tree where he had left his boots and outer garments. To descend that way was now impossible. He would have to circle around behind the mountain. Even though it was farther this way, it was the only safe alternative.

Mr. Dieu groped his way down the mountain for more than two hours before he reached the bottom. He had never had as difficult and as exhausting an ordeal as that. His body was covered in scratches. The monkey hovered between life and death, as he dragged it along the ground. For Mr. Dieu, it was agonizing to have to drag the monkey like that, but he no longer had the strength to carry it in his arms.

When Mr. Dieu reached the clump of bushes and vines he had hidden behind that morning, he stopped to pick up his hat and coat and the ball of sticky rice he had left there. But, to his astonishment, he found that a termites' nest as tall as rice stubble had risen in that spot. The nest was a sticky mound of fresh red earth plastered together with termites' wings. Unfortunately, his things had been mixed up in the nest and turned to mash. Mr. Dieu sighed, turned around in frustration, and lifted the monkey up in his arms. *How humiliating it will be to return home naked,* he scowled angrily. *I'll become a laughing stock.*

He set off, thinking about what he was going to do, and walked around in a circle until he found the track again. *How did this happen?* He burst out laughing. *Who has ever shot a monkey like this? A sparrow-and-a-half of meat on it. Golden hair like dye. You shoot an animal like this even though you've got no clothes? Serves you right, you old fool!*

There was a faint sound of something moving behind him. He gave a start, turned around, and recognized the female monkey, who immediately disappeared behind a bush. It turned out that she had followed Mr. Dieu from the mountain without his realizing it. *How bizarre,* he thought. After moving on for some distance, Mr. Dieu turned around again and, to his exasperation, saw that she was still following him. He put the male monkey down on the ground, gathered some stones, and chased the female monkey away. She gave a high-pitched scream and disappeared. When Mr. Dieu looked around a little later, she still tagged along behind him.

The trio continued to plod on through the jungle. The female monkey was incredibly persistent, and made Mr. Dieu feel that it was all so terribly unfair, that he was being pursued by misfortune.

By now, the male monkey had also recognized the call of his mate. He wriggled around. This wriggling made Mr. Dieu feel extremely wretched, and it so exhausted him that he didn't have the strength to carry the monkey any farther. To make matters worse, the monkey's hands clawed at Mr. Dieu's chest and made it bleed. Mr. Dieu could no longer bear the situation, and, in a fury, he threw the monkey down on the ground.

While the monkey lay sprawled out on a piece of wet grass, Mr. Dieu sat down and looked at it. Not far away, the female monkey bobbed out from behind the foot of a tree to see what was happening. As Mr. Dieu now looked at both of the monkeys, he felt a burning sensation on the bridge of his nose. Profoundly sad, he was overcome by the realization that, in life, responsibility weighs heavily on every living thing.

All right, I'll set you free, declared Mr. Dieu. He sat peacefully for a moment, then stood up without warning, and spat a wad of saliva on the ground near his feet. After hesitating for some time, he finally hurried off. The female monkey shot straight out of her hiding place as though she had been waiting for exactly this moment, and ran quickly to her mate.

Mr. Dieu turned onto another track because he wanted to avoid people. This track was choked with bramble bushes that made the going difficult, but they were covered by masses of *tu huyen* flowers. Mr. Dieu stopped in amazement. *Tu huyen* flowers bloom only once in thirty years, and people that come across them are said to meet with good luck. The flowers are white. They are as small as the head of a toothpick and have a salty taste. People call them "salt of the jungle." When the jungle is braided together with these flowers, it is a sign that the country is blessed with peace and abundant harvests.

When he came out of the valley, Mr. Dieu went down into the fields. The spring rain was gentle but very good for the rice seeds. Naked and lonely, he went on his way. A little later, his shadow faded into the curtain of rain.

In only a few days it would be the beginning of summer. The weather would gradually get warmer. . . .

Translated by Greg Lockhart

The Shelter

Duong Thu Huong

IT TOOK ME nineteen days to get through the defense lines. On the twentieth, the guide left me to my own devices.

"Here we are. This is the valley. From here on out you can go it alone. You can count on the locals for whatever you need. I've got to head back to camp; there's a delegation of psychological warfare experts waiting for me. I've got to guide them to our mountain bases. From here to Zone K the trail is really dangerous. Here's a map."

He fumbled in his pocket and produced a piece of crumpled paper; it was just an empty cigarette pack covered with marks and tiny letters.

"Thanks for all your help. Maybe we'll meet again?"

"Sure. I'll pick you up on the way back. I'm too tough and stringy to die. I've already survived 317 bombing raids."

I fished a can of meat out of my knapsack. "This is the last one I've got. You have it, comrade."

From *Novel without a Name*. Quan, a northern soldier who has been fighting for years without pause, has been given a short leave to return home.

14

The guide scrutinized it like a connoisseur. "This is a real luxury for an ordinary soldier. Good-bye, comrade."

He stuffed the can in his sack and turned to go. He had a pug nose and puffy red eyes, the kind of face they say brings bad luck. There was something sinister about him. But then he was just a faithful guide, by all appearances a gentle, decent man. God bless him. After all, he had survived 317 bombardments.

The sun shone like a ball of fire. The guide disappeared into the forest. I walked toward a strip of grass, an open space of endless green and light. And when I lay down, I let myself go, drifting toward a feeling I had forgotten. At last I was free from the suffocating atmosphere of the forest, its stifling shadows of dense vegetation, its poisonous fragrances that sent shivers up my spine.

Above my head, the sky was an uninterrupted blue. Cloudless. The grass stretched out in front of me as far as the eye could see. The dew soaked into my clothes. Prickly grasses tickled me, scratching my feet, my legs. I could feel the sun burning into my scalp, my back, the shaved nape of my neck. A delicious warmth washed over my head, my body, in a million droplets of light. I felt my pale skin redden in the sun; the pleasure of it, just being alive. I rolled over. The sky beamed red through my eyelids. My cheeks, my neck, my chest, my arms, everything was gently warmed. The sun flooded me like a tide. I remained a long time like that, without moving, without sleeping, floating in a half-conscious state. Memories glided across my dazzled eyelids. There were faces, landscapes, murmurings, laughter. They seemed to float in smoke, pierced by a long, thin shaft of light, like a sparkling thread of glass. I had never known happiness. So was this it, just this moment? I had never known freedom. Maybe this was it. Just this instant. Who would ever understand? Words, words are as slippery as eels. Just when you think you grasp them, they slide out of your hands and disappear into the mud. But these grasses, razor-sharp at my side, this blue sky above my head, this was real. I was happy.

I stayed stretched out like that for a long time. The ground beneath me was scorching now; the dew had evaporated and the grass had turned a deeper shade of green. The sound of an airplane rumbled overhead. I didn't care. Why bother running for cover? I thought: Bullets may miss people, but no one dodges a bullet. I got up and looked at the carpet of grass. It had been ten years since I had seen such beauty. What miracle had allowed this patch to survive so many bombings? It had an unreal beauty, like a satin ribbon discarded along a shattered, bumpy road of the war.

Planes howled across the sky. I remained buried in the high grass. The grass protected me; at the very least, its green tenderness soothed my soul. The planes veered toward the southwest, glinting in the sun. A carpet of bombs gushed forth. They tilted toward the ground, gently, calmly. Falling toward the earth, they looked like a cloud of giant termites, their wings sheared off.

The cataclysm lasted about half an hour. Then the forest and the mountain sank back into silence. The sun was dazzling at its zenith. The ground around me was hot and gave off a dense, steamy vapor. I undid my knapsack, drank a bit of water, ate some dried provisions I had, and returned to the road. The prairie was much more vast than I had imagined. I struggled across what seemed like a sea of grass. At dusk, I reached the footpath through the forest marked N22 on the map. About three hundred yards down the path I saw a board bearing a cross and the word SHELTER. Map in hand, I walked toward it. After about four hundred paces, the footpath widened into a courtyard paved with wood and sheet metal cannibalized from old trucks. At the back of the courtyard, a small stone staircase led to another shelter hollowed out from the rock. I cupped my hand around my mouth and shouted: "Hey, anyone there?"

In the still air of the forest, my voice echoed, bouncing lugubriously off the rocks. Another voice responded immediately: "Just a minute . . ."

What luck, I thought. I took off my hat, wiped my face with my handkerchief, and waited. Ten minutes passed. I could hear the heavy tread of footsteps. A hulking, shadowy figure approached. Night had already fallen, and I couldn't make out the features of its face. "Greetings, comrade. I've come from the third line of the front. Could you offer me shelter for the night? I'll be off at dawn."

The shadow answered me in a rasping voice: "You could be a deserter. Show me your papers."

I chuckled: "No, I'm no deserter. I'm on a mission to Zone K. Here, here are my papers."

The shadow lit a battery-powered lamp. A tiny sliver of light illuminated my mission order and my army ID card. Then I saw the face: a flat square, cheeks covered with red pimples, buckteeth protruding over thick, horsy lips. The light suddenly went out. A puffy hand stuffed the papers back into mine. The rasping voice continued: "Follow me, elder brother."

A woman. It's a woman! I almost said it aloud. She had turned away from me, guiding me toward the shelter. The lamp glowed intermittently, sweeping over the crumbling steps.

"Be careful. The other day a guy from Lao Cai fell and broke four teeth."

"Thanks, comrade," I murmured.

"Here we are," she said, pulling me through a wooden door. "Wait a minute. That's strange—I'm sure I left the lighter here somewhere. Ah, here it is."

A sudden pop. Light poured out as the woman lit another lamp: It must have burned on a mixture of gasoline and salt, judging from the thick smoke it gave off. I looked around. There was a bed made of munitions crates covered with tenting fabric. Tacked to the wall were a tin can, a tiny mirror decorated with a paper flower, and photos of famous Parisian singers and movie stars.

"It's awfully bright. Won't the planes be able to spot us?"

"Impossible. We're perfectly safe here. As for the gasoline, don't worry about that. I get a steady supply from the truck drivers."

She disappeared toward the back of the shelter and came back with some empty munitions crates.

"What are you doing, comrade?" I asked.

"Your bed. Here you go. Empty crates. We've got as many as you want."

"Thanks, but I've got my hammock."

"A hammock? You might as well go sleep in the forest.

As long as you're here, it's silly to sleep in a hammock."
She arranged the crates to make a smooth surface, then
pulled one of the tent shells off the wall. "Here, stretch
this out. I've got to go to the cave to get some wood."

"What cave?" I asked.

"At the back of the shelter. It's a kind of storage space,"
she answered, shuffling off. The darkness engulfed her
massive, bearlike body. I could hear the sound of wood
splitting as I spread the tent shells over the crates. I
propped my knapsack and my rifle in a corner of the
room and sat down, stretching out my exhausted legs. A
tongue of flame ran down my thighs to the tips of my
toes.

The woman reappeared, a bundle of logs in her arms.
She knelt by the hearth and the flames cruelly lit up her
face. I shuddered, she was hideous. She looked up at me:
"I'll put a pot of rice on. You stay here and watch it. I'm
going to go take a quick bath in the river, then I'll be
back."

I looked at the pitch-black night outside. "At this
hour?"

"I'm used to it. I've got to wash."

Just then I noticed that her uniform was stained with
something like black mud; she gave off a nauseating,
sweaty odor.

"What's that on your clothes? Blood?"

"Yes, it's blood. I've wrestled hand-to-hand with three
corpses since noon."

"What do you mean?"

She smiled weakly and then pursed her lips. Her nose
twitched slightly as she spoke: "What about it? I'm in
charge of N22 Cemetery. My job is to gather corpses in

these parts. All the unidentified ones are behind the hill. They're all combatants. Just like the three who were killed by this morning's bombing. I buried them all myself. The cave at the back of this shelter is a stockhouse for their belongings. I pass them along to the army when they come through."

She turned, took the lid off an aluminum pot near the fire, and poured in some water through a hollowed-out bamboo trunk. Then she dipped into an old egg-powder canister and measured out some rice. "Don't wash the rice or it'll lose its bran," she lectured me. "If you catch scurvy, it's all over. You can forget about finding medicine here."

She raised herself off her knees. "You make the rice. Here's the lighter. Use the pinewood for kindling. It lights in a flash. The water will boil in seconds."

She grabbed some clothes from under the bed and rushed outside. I heard the gravel crunch under her feet. I chopped up a plank of pine and lit the fire. I stacked a few logs on it and watched the pot. The water began to boil and slowly evaporate. The rice was cooked by the time she returned. She had changed into clean clothes and rolled her hair into a tight chignon on top of her head. As she wrung out her wet clothes, she shot a glance in my direction: "Spread the coals, otherwise it's going to burn."

I obeyed her mechanically. Meanwhile, she hung her laundry out to dry on a metal wire strung up near the fire. A strange odor filled the room. When I started to sniff, she tossed her head, unfurling her wet hair onto her neck.

"I haven't had soap for three months. Without soap, you'd need a miracle to get rid of the smell of blood. Build up the fire; the smoke will cover the smell. You'll get used to it."

She combed out her hair. Her caressing, feminine gestures jarred with her hulking, wrestler's body. I tossed a few more logs on the fire and kept my eyes fixed on the flames.

The fog had rolled in and a few wisps hovered in the cool darkness. The woman sat down beside me. Her soft, shiny black hair streamed down her back. She placed a tiny pot over the fire and dropped a lump of lard into it. "I want you to taste some vegetables sautéed in MSG. I found them this morning, just before those bastards started bombing us. There's even a can of meat. Just over a pound, enough to really eat your fill." She threw a handful of wild chilies and a bit of salt into the pot and stirred it rapidly, like you stir grilled paddy rice. Then she pulled the pot off the fire: "Put the vegetables in your mess dish."

I obeyed her like a child. She got up abruptly and went off into the cave, returning with a can of meat.

"It's imported from China. 'The Queen of Canned Meat'—you're probably familiar with it. There's no fat."

She placed the can by the side of the fire. My heart jumped. I recognized the can I had given to the guide that morning, the knife mark on the lid. Luong had given it to me before my departure. I had wanted to offer it to his soldiers as a treat, but he had stopped me, muttering that it wasn't considered normal to offer such fare to foot soldiers. The knife mark on the lid was from an American penknife I'd borrowed from Luong's aide-de-camp.

"Where did you find this?" I couldn't help asking the obvious question. The woman looked at me, surprised: "They told me I could eat whatever food I found on the

. . . I keep a list of the belongings I find in their knapsacks. You've probably never seen anything like it. I'll show you—they're odd, rather funny. Some of them collect dozens of handkerchiefs, underwear, bras for their sweethearts back home. Others carry around stones or acorns with their friends' names carved into them. Every soldier is different. As for the diaries, most of them are in shreds. Anyway, let's eat, I'm hungry."

She pried open the can of meat and pushed it in front of me. She filled a bowl with rice and set it in my hand, just as a wife would do for her husband. Awkwardly, I murmured my thanks.

She didn't answer, just lowered her head and started eating. I realized that she was waiting for something, something more tender, but my tongue froze. I ate with my head lowered. Silence fell between us. Time passed. I heard it passing with the crackle of the flames. Suddenly, she raised her head: "Why are you just eating the vegetables? Are you too good to eat canned meat?"

"I've got stomach problems. For a long time now I've only eaten rice."

"You can't find bamboo shoots back where you come from?"

"Sometimes, but it's rare."

She served me another bowl of rice. Little by little the atmosphere grew less tense.

"You men are so lazy. There are bamboo shoots in every forest. There's never any shortage of vegetables."

"It's true. We male soldiers are useless, not like you."

"You call us she-soldiers, don't you? What a bunch of bastards . . . What's your name, anyway? I didn't catch it."

"Quan. My name is Quan."

"What a lovely name. I'm Vieng. Have another bowl of rice. Or have you had enough? With your appetite, you can't be much of a heavyweight in combat. Even I eat two bowls more than you do."

"Thank you, comrade."

"'Thank you' this, 'thank you' that—what hypocrisy! You must be from Hanoi."

"I come from the village of Dong Tien."

"You sure don't look like a villager. I'd say you've turned your back on your roots. Here, taste some of this burned-rice juice. It's very refreshing. Leave the bowls and the chopsticks. I'll wash them tomorrow. Let's sleep. I'm exhausted."

She drank her bowl in one gulp, stretched out on the bed, and began to snore almost at once. Her head rested on a little white pillow. One of the red threads had started to come loose. She slept with her mouth open, her teeth pointing toward the sky. I sneaked a sidelong glance at her. She filled me with a mixture of horror, curiosity, and pity. I closed the door and climbed onto my own bed. I sank into sleep, a deep, restful sleep.

I didn't dream. I woke up feeling a weight on my stomach, and I knew instantly that it was her, that she had come to press herself up against me. Her hair brushed over my shoulder, her huge arm circled my stomach. She seemed hesitant. I felt her warm breathing, and from time to time, she shifted and heaved a sigh, murmuring something. I lay totally still, feigning sleep. But all my senses were on alert, as tense as radar before an air attack. I knew that she was watching me, waiting for my slightest movement.

At the foot of the bed the coals still glowed, and the

heat comforted me. The light exposed me, and I kept my eyes firmly closed. She shifted violently; I could hear her panting. Suddenly, impatiently, she shook me by the belt. I grumbled, pretending to sleep, and rolled over. That was a mistake: She knew immediately that I was awake. She called my name: "Quan."

I didn't respond. She said my name again: "Quan?" I kept silent. She let go of my belt and sat up in bed. "Quan, why are you so cruel? I'm all alone here. It's terrible. Open your eyes. Listen to me."

I didn't dare open my eyes. I turned over and spoke to her softly: "Comrade Vieng, it's because you're alone here that I want to spare you trouble. If by accident you got . . . it would kill you."

She let out a little cry and threw herself onto me: "There's no risk. If I got pregnant from you, all the better. Quan, come, Quan."

She began to moan. I said, "Comrade Vieng, get hold of yourself. You have to control yourself or you're going to make a fatal mistake."

"No, no," she moaned softly. "But I want to die. Take me, kill me, make me die."

She pulled me against her, lifted me onto her.

I felt paralyzed by a strange sensation. *Just close your eyes,* I said to myself. *Let's get this over with. Close your eyes.* I felt my arms and legs grow numb. Throbbing terror, a fascinating desire. I heard her pant, cry out, "Quan, darling, darling."

I saw her by the red light of the coals, her eyes closed, her large mouth agape, stammering, panting. Nonsense words gushed from her horrible teeth. "Quan, darling, kill me, kill me."

Her cry of agony aroused a morbid feeling in me that entirely drowned my desire; all at once I felt totally lucid. My face burned with shame. I pushed her away and sat up. "Comrade Vieng, we mustn't."

She jumped to my side: "Quan, you think I'm ugly, don't you? Do you want me to put out the fire?" She rushed to the fire, grabbed a log, and proceeded to crush the coals with a hurried, but careful stroke. I stared at her stooped body and moved closer to her. "Come sit down. I can explain."

She followed me obediently, gazing up at me with docile, consenting eyes. Each feature of her crude face— her pug nose, her low forehead, her buckteeth—looked neglected, pleaded for pleasure with an expectancy that was as much a female animal's as it was a woman's. Why didn't I have the courage of a To Vu? Stranded on an island during a journey, he had slept with a monkey. Why didn't I have this ancient king's resolve, his compassion? Out of respect for a certain woman's dignity, he had made her a queen, despite the hideousness of her face. These rare men, had they been sages or wild beasts?

"Listen to me, comrade Vieng." I took her hand to maintain a distance between us, to protect myself. I forced myself to look at her directly, to spare her any shame.

"Please don't be angry with me. I don't want to hurt you, but really, I can't . . ."

She looked at me, her voice quavering, stammering my name.

"Do you understand? I just can't," I repeated.

She gave me a suspicious look. Suddenly, she plunged her hand between my thighs. The investigation was conclusive; she could feel for herself that I was useless. She withdrew her hand and stared at me in silence, her eyes soft, pitying. It was my turn to be pitied. *Saved,* I thought to myself with relief. "Look, please understand me—I didn't mean to . . ." I stammered.

She got up and angrily tossed her head. "It's probably all those chemicals. Those American bastards!" Then she turned toward me. "Go on, try to get some sleep. You've got a long way to go tomorrow."

She returned to her bed, but I couldn't sleep anymore. I added a few logs to the fire, rekindling it. I watched, hypnotized, like an old gibbon staring at the sun.

My relief had evaporated. All I felt now was bitterness. I was innocent, but still sorry for the lie. Despite myself, shame overwhelmed me. It crawled like an invisible fungus growing in my brain, its pale, poisonous shadow seeping slowly into my body. My thoughts jumped about frantically: Was I a coward? Impotent? A man so lacking in virility that he ran from the chance for a wild coupling? Was I selfish, so lacking in humanity that I could not even respond to her as an animal would? I felt enslaved by centuries of prejudice and ignorance. Dreams of purity— outdated values, lost in an existence steeped in mud and blood—or else . . . I didn't dare follow my thoughts. I had rejected a woman who had welcomed me simply and warmly, who had begged me for a moment of happiness, a moment of life, of the life we had all lost a long time ago and that we remembered now only intermittently, in sudden flashes and premonitions. Or was she just too hideous? No, it couldn't have been only that.

She had dragged three corpses in the sunset. She had closed the eyes of three dead men. Alone, she had buried them on the other side of the hill. She lived here, guarding their belongings, keeping watch over their shadows, these mementos of life.

This woman was born of the war. She belonged to it, had been forged by it. It wasn't just because she was ugly that I had rejected her—I had been afraid to face myself, scared of the truth. I was a coward. Ten years of war had gone by. I had known both glory and humiliation, lived through all its sordid games. I had needed to meet her to finally see myself clearly. I had been defeated from the beginning. The eighteen-year-old boy who had thrown himself into army life was still just a boy, wandering, lost out there, somewhere just beyond the horizon. I had never really committed myself to war.

The fire burned brighter and brighter, its light seeping into the corners of the shelter, its gentle warmth enveloping everything. The woman had gone back to sleep, her breathing was regular, rhythmic, and one of her arms lay over her forehead. Pensive, I watched her. With all my heart I wished her luck. Surely, there were men somewhere, truly born of this war, who would bring her the happiness she deserved. I scribbled a few words of thanks in the notebook that listed the belongings of the dead. I gathered my own belongings and left. It was 4:32. The night was freezing, pitch-black. I looked the map over carefully, and when I had committed its contours to memory, I headed off, groping my way.

Translated by Phan Huy Duong and Nina McPherson

The Saigon Tailor Shop

Pham Thi Hoai

THE SAIGON Tailor Shop isn't in Saigon or in California. I was standing at the railroad crossing on Kham Thien Street, waiting for the train to go by. The handlebar of my bicycle got caught in the basket of the sidewalk cigarette seller, and she called me a certain animal name; it was then that I noticed the huge sign above her head: SAIGON TAILOR SHOP, SEWING CLASSES, ALL STYLES FOR MEN AND WOMEN, LATEST FASHION, and in parentheses below, SUITS, JACKETS, TRADITIONAL TUNICS.

When I met Dung that night, I told him I was going to learn sewing. He said, "No, no. You've done French, English, computers, and bridal makeup." We each had a glass of sugarcane juice. For some reason, Dung also asked for a Vina cigarette, and I ordered a plate of sunflower seeds. When I finished the seeds and Dung his cigarette, he said, "I'm telling you, one career, certain success." I said, "This time, I am sticking to one career." Dung said, "I beg you, you keep saying 'this time.'"

When I went into the tailor shop, I saw a group of twenty girls, all from the countryside, sitting at the sewing machines, no one paying attention to me. I wanted to turn around and leave, but the cigarette seller had blocked my bicycle in, and asking her to let me pass by was to become another animal, and besides, someone called out, "Hey, girl, what's your name? Want to learn?" It was the owner, squeezing her stomach and her ass through, in between the girls. She was flipping through a dog-eared notebook and said, "One hundred and twenty western and traditional styles for men and women latest fashion beginners two hundred and fifty intermediate four hundred both beginner and intermediate six hundred—that's a discount of fifty—advanced means cutting directly on fabric traditional tunics or suits with credible teachers now what is your name?"

"Now what is your name?" I thought she must be real busy and my induction ceremony had to be that quick, with an avalanche so extremely clear. Later I called her Ms. Snow, and once in a while I also called her Mamma, just like the rest of her students. I was obviously a Hanoi woman, so the whole group called me Older Sister and referred to themselves as Younger Sisters. I found out on the second day that there were four instructors: two males, one on the floor above, teaching cutting techniques; two other males below teaching sewing; and, in addition, the owner's daughter specialized in seam stitching, two daughters-in-law were responsible for all kinds of tasks, and another woman, also from the countryside, took care of meals.

There was nothing I could see that was Saigon about the place. Once I sat down at the Chinese sewing machine, learning to use the ends of the scissors to make lines, I thought I could still run off. The French and English and computer courses were full of urban, educated people, and rich, or at least people pretending to be rich and polite. The bridal makeup class was also civilized. In comparison, the Saigon Tailor Shop was a dark train car packed with dreams, and I had bought an express ticket to a future full of cheap dress shirts and windbreakers with fake South Korean labels. That night, Dung asked me how the class went. I said, "It's great. In three months I could open my own shop." I thought that the first thing I'd make would be a pair of shorts. I'd wrap them in newspaper, making sure Dung would not try them on until he was home.

I couldn't believe the names of the twenty girls: Doggie, Green, Bamboo, Luck, Escape, Perfumed, Soaked, North. The boss was Snow; her daughter was Touched; the two daughters-in-law were Chalk and Virtue; the four teachers were Determined, Leg, Fight, and Win. All day upstairs, there were shouts about dividing the hip, adding the chest, subtracting the armpit, hip, chest, armpit. Downstairs it was impossible to hear a word; even if you shouted, the ceiling fan would cut your words into meaningless bits and pieces. I thought I'd end up in the Tran Quy mental hospital before I got to making shorts. That's why when the girl told me her name was Orchid, I liked her right away. In other places, all the Orchids were boring. But this one wasn't like the rest of the girls in the shop.

She was sitting next to me, her bamboo-shoot fingers sweet as honey, mocking my uneven lines of threads, when her father came from the countryside into the store. Ms. Snow asked him, "Are you here to buy a dress shirt or a pair of elastic pants or do you want to register your daughter for classes?" Orchid's father said, "No, I wouldn't dare," and then he started to tell his sad story about looking for a daughter who'd gone to Hanoi to learn sewing and it had been six months but she hadn't returned. Ms. Snow said, "Dear Uncle, Hanoi has hundreds of tailor shops." Her father replied: "This is the nineteenth store I've come to." He had already turned to leave when Ms. Snow said: "Well, what's her name maybe?"

"We call her Tiny at home."

Orchid crawled out from under the table and told me, "That's my Daddy." I didn't like her real name.

In the beginning, I thought I was the worst of the class and concentrated on learning. First you learn to sew in straight lines, then you do collars, then sleeves. On the third day Ms. Snow told me to go upstairs to learn the basics of making a dress shirt. Professors Determined and Leg taught the whole bunch without much organization. Whoever called out for the professors would get them to come; otherwise Professor Determined, a young man, would just spread himself out on the table and sing, while Professor Leg swung his legs and shot the breeze. Professor Determined was shirtless. Professor Leg's shirt was unbuttoned and revealed his bulging stomach. Professor Determined was good-looking. Professor Leg was a teacher at the School of Fine Arts and spoke about stuff none of the students could believe. Professor Determined primarily taught the basics of cutting. Professor Leg showed how to modify a cut to make it more artsy-fartsy. When I got upstairs, Orchid was trying out a pink overcoat, and Professor Leg was forever rubbing the chest, saying it was still wrinkled and needed recutting, then he said, "Excuse me," putting his hand inside to check on the lining. Professor Determined, who was singing some folk songs, jumped up and said, "This coat would go great with that seven-piece dress. It would kill!" Professor Leg said, "Oh no, the seven-piece dress is peasant style.

Orchid must wear a white skirt up to here." He put his hands together and made a circle on her legs, continuing, "Excuse me, no one here knows anything about aesthetics. It's really sad."

I stuck with Professor Determined's basic styles. According to his way of cutting, everything was the same. You add a little to the chest on a woman's blouse, a lower cut on a man's shirt, and for kids, you don't worry about taking in the sides. This way, I learned over ten styles in one day; I could probably do a hundred and twenty styles in ten days.

After the basic shirts, we moved on to basic trousers. "The shirts ought to be in linden green, and the trousers in purple," Ms. Snow instructed. "That way you can sell them to peasants." In addition to the tailor shop, she was also the manager of the Ascending Dragon Poetry Club, of which the two downstairs professors, Fight and Win, were also members. They were both old, and often told us that it took time and patience to be a tailor; this was no joke.

One day Ms. Snow grabbed the *New Hanoi* newspaper and sang out a poem. I'd just caught some line that went "green blades of grass playing with the bridge of friendship," when Ms. Snow shouted: "Damn why did they type in friendship where it should have been love Touched where are you go straight to the newspaper office make them run a correction these are my words they ain't no joke!" Both professors Fight and Win nodded their heads; that's right, friendship makes no sense. The Ascending Dragon Club's certificate of honor was hanging on the wall among the collar samples. You had to look for it or you wouldn't see it.

Whatever happened, I didn't run away from the place. After the sewing episode was over, like the French and English and computer and bridal makeup classes, I went back to my office and read the newspapers as usual, thinking that perhaps I would take a secretarial-managerial course next, but the tailor shop, that train car full of dreams next to the railroad crossing on Kham Thien Street, stayed on my mind. Sitting at my sewing machine almost out on the sidewalk, I had thought that when the Unification Train crawled past here, you could hook this dark car onto it and drag it all the way to Saigon. The real Saigon. There the girls would have new names. The girls who had abandoned their villages with the hope of creating fashion out of baby-blue and purple fabrics would learn more than a hundred and twenty styles, and I could say good-bye to Dung from a position of strength. Here I was hoping he would marry me, but it hadn't happened. He was practical. If we both sat reading the newspaper at two offices, we couldn't have a family. I wasn't asking that outside of his official job; Dung had to know about fixing TVs or washing motorcycles. But he had demands. I thought our traditions were that women had to work hard, so I took the sewing class.

After a week, the instructors complimented me on my intelligence. I could correctly divide the hip, add the chest, and subtract the armpit. Many of the girls hadn't finished fourth grade and couldn't do it. Orchid finished tenth grade, and was certainly unlike the rest. The rest of them were obsessed with the dresses that had layered collars and pleated sleeves that looked like lanterns about to float up in the air. I often had to model for their cheery styles, baggy, quarter-cut, bat-winged, flaring skirts, German collar, Japanese collar . . . they used my urban silhouette as an example, then they would fight to try things on, all day long they were putting things on, taking things off, standing half-naked in front of the shop, and whatever shyness, whatever shame they had, they sent it all back to their Mammas and Daddys in the villages.

One day Orchid told me that there was a suit downtown that cost nine hundred thousand; the labor for it must cost eight hundred thousand. In the country, even the most stylish person would only spend twenty thousand on a dress, and the labor would be around five thousand, but that's still better than working the land. After finishing the pink overcoat, Orchid made a white skirt right to the line Professor Leg had marked on her legs. Professor Leg told her she had taste. When Ms. Snow saw her coming downstairs, zipping through the shop to go out, proudly looking like a pink piece of chalk hemmed in white, she cried, "You'd better pay me the rest of your tuition fees you hear?" Orchid turned and tilted her head just like an actress on stage and said, "Mamma, don't you worry, I am not about to stick my head under a train." Ms. Snow turned to the rest of the students, "If I had known this I would have turned her over to her father poor old man what kind of daughter is that what is she learning here nothing but to be such a sassy thing."

From where I was sitting at my machine next to the sidewalk, I could see Orchid slipping through the railroad bars, dancing on the tracks. Her high heels got stuck. She fell but didn't bother to get up, just stayed right there and showed her teeth to the advancing black train. The next day she told me, "I don't have to avoid the train, it will avoid me." I had no self-confidence left after trying my luck with the French and English and computer and bridal makeup courses, so I respected the girl's blind conviction. She was using this tailor shop as a starting point. I was stopping here. Our friendship was as short as our luck. In two months, I got nothing out of her but her fake name. She got nothing out of me either. What the girl needed most was to unload the stuff she was carrying inside of her. But to put that sad story into me was like putting a difficult thread through the eye of a needle. That's why Orchid stayed put upstairs, only zipping through the bottom floor to go out each night with a new dress. Pouring her soul out to Professor Leg was like pouring gold into its mold; add to that Professor Determined's beautiful mouth and corny songs, so Orchid would come to me with her bamboo-shoot fingers only to ask what "fantasy" meant. Off she went. Whatever was left of her story, she poured it into clothes.

Once, I too went out to dance on the tracks when the railroad barriers were down. That night I told Dung that it was a thrill. I didn't need to avoid the train, it was avoiding me. After our glasses of sugarcane juice, Dung suddenly kissed me. Our tongues were as sweet as honey candy and our lips matched fine, and I had to fight hard to free mine and tell him that if we were to get married, the money people would give us would probably be enough to buy a sewing machine. Dung said, "I beg you, you keep saying, 'if, if . . .'"

I thought it was time to make a pair of shorts so I took some fabric upstairs to ask Professor Leg for help. It was no special fabric, but perhaps Professor Leg could do some fantasy on the style. There was no one else upstairs except for Professor Determined, who was lying on his back on the table, directly beneath the ceiling fan, patting his stomach and singing. Some of his hair was swimming in a bowl of soup left on the table. He asked, "What are you cutting?" I said, "Shorts." He said, "Basic cuts, shorter legs." I thought they wouldn't be much without some fantasy designs, so I used their meal as an excuse to leave. But Professor Determined sat up and said, "Let me see," and then went, *snip, snip* with the scissors, and then went back to lying down, his hair in the soup again.

Downstairs, Ms. Snow was having a crisis. The month before, she had had another one. One of her two grand-children was fourteen months old and often crawled around beneath the tables. Once in a while he would get stuck between our pedals, and we would have to hear him screaming and crying for a while. This time he had put a couple of needles into his mouth and didn't spit them out until Ms. Snow gave him some soybean milk. Whenever Ms. Snow had a crisis, the girls stopped taking things off and putting things on, and whoever was without pants was without luck. The two daughters-in-law went up-stairs, one on the left, one on the right above our heads. They took turns throwing words back at their mother-in-law and mocked each other. On the ground, in the air, were fighting words, words about one's private parts now being forced down each other's throats. The daughter stitching seams in the middle of the room would let fly a bitter comment once in a while.

That day I became convinced there was an artistic temperament in this tailor shop. Of the two instructors up-stairs, one was a singer; the other, a master of aesthetics.

Downstairs there was poetry, and once in a while, a crisis. When I came down with the freshly cut shorts in my hands, the girls were holding on to Ms. Snow's stomach so that it wouldn't explode, but there was no one who could hold her mouth. Normally her extremely clear sentences would sooner or later find a stop. Now in this moment of crisis, they just wouldn't end. You had to be a part of that tailor shop. The women selling cigarettes and Russian electric wares from across the street rushed over, but they couldn't get much out of it. I came down from upstairs and walked right into the middle of her sentence: ". . . no cleaning leaving the iron plugged in it's like you just shit right there leave it to this old bitch to clean it all up I get to carry this big stomach around to serve you young whores and what are you learning but to be sassy and you can't sew in a straight line buttons hanging out all over the place like cunts buttonholes full of threads watch it or I'll chase all of you out of here this is a decent business people here are educated they know poetry properly this ain't a whorehouse it ain't the kind of whorehouse you can just walk in and out anytime you like this is not a market this day and age who's feeding who and if not me then let the dogs love you. . . ."

I stood right there inside her sentence and didn't want to leave for suddenly I felt really happy; my life, in all aspects, compared to Ms. Snow's, was a series of good luck. My waist measured just twenty-four-and-a-half inches, and I spoke a kind of language that was slow and had periods. The shorts, cut by Professor Determined to be just the basic shorts with no creativity, were just a small tragedy. Perhaps Orchid could sew them together and salvage them for me. Her seam lines were always sweet as a drawing. Orchid appeared from somewhere just now, Professor Leg in tow. She took off upstairs, Professor Leg stayed behind. His stomach and Ms. Snow's were apt opponents. He said, "Sister, don't let people laugh at you." Ms. Snow went on with her scary modern poem, derailing herself for just a moment to make an aside, "You think just because you are talented you can do whatever you want I pay your salary to teach or go to cafés this isn't a whorehouse this is not a market. . . ." Orchid came down. She was wearing her favorite, the pink overcoat and the white miniskirt. High heels. Lipstick. Hair like a waterfall. She dropped down step by step, stopping on each, her legs parting and closing, mesmerizing. Halting in front of Ms. Snow, she said, "Mamma, you don't stop, I'm going to put my head in front of the train."

Ms. Snow wanted to, but couldn't. When she had a crisis, her avalanches just wouldn't stop. Orchid rushed out on the streets, crawled through the barriers, and placed herself across the tracks. When we all heard the screeching brakes and ran out, it was too late. She was cut into three, the mesmerizing legs pointing toward the shop, her hair falling toward the flower shops. Her coat and her skirt were red. You could only see the pink and the white if you looked close enough. Maybe she had faced the sky. Above her were the traffic lights tied to the electric cables. She had probably been smiling and calculating: one, two, three, Ms. Snow is going to stop. One, two, three, someone's coming for me. . . .

The girl had only been in Hanoi for six months, she couldn't have known that here nobody cared to get in-

volved. Even if I had been there just beyond the barriers,
I would have merely opened my eyes wider to look. This
time the train didn't avoid her. This was the Unification
Train on an express run to Saigon. Still owing her tuition
fees, Orchid could now leave the three pieces of her body
in Hanoi and send her soul, without paying the fare, directly to Saigon. She could use her real name there. No
way her father would find her there. I remembered that
someone had said, if a Saigon girl is beautiful, it will be
the modern, boisterous kind of beauty. A beautiful Hanoi
girl would have a classic, aristocratic kind of beauty.
Orchid possessed nothing classic or aristocratic. She had
to leave Hanoi. Hanoi couldn't appreciate her enthusiastic and rather crazy way of decorating herself.

The tailor shop closed down for a day to deal with the
funeral. Orchid had no resident paper in town, and no
one knew anything about her village, so Ms. Snow
adopted her so she could bury her in the city's cemetary,
Van Dien. She brought flowers and incense all the way
out the railroad tracks. Each time the train ran past,
the flowers and incense would be crushed. She would
bring out new flowers and incense, dozens of times a day.
She would hit herself on the face to ask for Orchid's for-
giveness. Each day she would hit herself dozens of times,
to pay for a mean mouth, but not a mean heart. Inside the
tailor shop, the girls pushed against each other, holding
their breath, and looked at her. They'd never seen anything so full of suspense their whole life. I felt that
Orchid, floating around in the South, would have to turn
back to Hanoi once in a while to show her compassion.
Professor Leg said that day he had taken her to the

School of Fine Arts for a visit. There was a School of
Design there. They had then sat in a café, talking over
how he would first find a way for her to become a
painter's model. He didn't go out to the tracks to light incense, but he lay down next to Professor Determined and
cried: "My dear, why such fatal self-respect?" I thought I
had no self-respect left after the times I suggested marriage to Dung, so I feared the blind self-respect of the
young girl. Every once in a while I would be terrified that
she would come back to Hanoi, not because of Ms.
Snow's self-mortification, but just to ask me what
"Design" meant.

The next day, I brought the shorts back to get them
sewn. There were nine machines downstairs, but only one
that wouldn't break the threads, and whoever got it first
wouldn't let go. That day, the downstairs was deserted. I
lowered the needle on my fabric and claimed the machine
before going upstairs. The girls had surrounded Professor
Leg and demanded pink overcoats. One for each of them.
I thought they had all gone crazy. The way it was going,
the twenty white mini-skirts were coming next, and my
urban silhouette was surely going to be the model again.
Twenty times I'd be the meaningless piece of pink chalk,
hemmed in white. Then they would all change their
names at the same time, throwing the old ones under the
table like broken needles for the fourteen-month-old kid
to chew on. I told myself to remain calm, not wishing for
a chance to visit the School of Fine Arts like them, but to
simply go downstairs and finish making the shorts. Cut
the threads. Iron. Unplug the iron. Stick the elastic band
through. When I was done, I wrapped the shorts care-

fully in the newspaper that had the news about Orchid. I'd ask Dung not to open the package until he got home. I knew these shorts were as ugly as this crossroad with the railroad tracks.

The next day I walked in right on top of the girls' pink-and-white putting-on, taking-off session. Ms. Snow, her daughter, the two daughters-in-law, the maid, and all four instructors were watching like zombies, and the bunch of female butterflies seemed to have taken opium. Even the rats in the alley leading to the market seemed to have opium feet. I finished my role as a model for twenty pink-and-white outfits and was about to leave when Ms. Snow handed me a newspaper package, "What's-his-name left this." Dung's note simply said "Thank you but I have no need for this at the moment." Last night our tongues had again been sweet as honey candy and our lips matched fine. I didn't free my lips to talk about marriage. I knew it would be our last kiss.

I was thinking of asking Ms. Snow for a refund of my tuition, telling her that I had to go somewhere immediately on assignment. Perhaps to Saigon. But she was in a crisis again and I couldn't cut her off. She was bowing to the pink-and-white girls who were dancing in the streets. "Mamma begs you I eat grass eat hay you lived wisely died divine Orchid my dear Tiny my dear please don't dance I beg you."

I walked down the street, thinking I was on assignment to Saigon. Next I might be taking a secretarial-managerial course.

Translated by Nguyen Qui Duc

The Goat Meat Special

Ho Anh Thai

NOT ONLY did Hoi finally manage to buy a television, it was even a color set.

One evening his two little devils went to visit their grandparents, and his wife slunk off to meet with her boss, the manager of the Ban Toc government hotel. Hoi wondered why she was sneaking in and out of the house so much these days. The campaign against corruption was in full swing all over the country—perhaps the two of them were covering something up. Left alone in the house, Hoi turned on the television and grabbed a mystery novel. He read inattentively, listening with half an ear to the TV. His eyes swept up from the book when a fashion show came on the screen. The models appeared to be amateurs, their movements exaggerated and artificial, their arms flapping loosely. They tripped clumsily over their own feet like puppets jerked by strings. The last model was a girl in a two-piece bathing suit. She threw a clumsily seductive look at the camera, turned to display her back, and turned again. Suddenly something unprecedented occurred. The model tore off her top, dropped it at her feet and began turning round and round. Hoi shouted at the screen, trying to cue her that she wasn't in her bathroom. But it was too late. The girl had already stripped to her birthday suit. A sequence of totally nude shots followed.

Hoi couldn't believe that television was getting so progressive and bold. But since it was unbelievable, he told himself to be very cautious when he inquired about it. The next morning, while everybody else in the office was exchanging gossip, Hoi casually asked, "That TV program last night was quite rousing, wasn't it?"

"It was ridiculous," a young man quacked at Hoi. "Whenever they were about to kiss, the camera skimmed off over trees or houses or trains to avoid it. That kind of film should be reserved only for pensioners and old managers' clubs."

"Nonsense!" Dien, their general manager, snapped. "To the contrary, we only like entirely open movies—the kind where anything on the girls' bodies gets entirely opened. But we're too experienced and dedicated to be corrupted by such films," he said severely, admonishing the younger man. "While you . . . better to be cautious. If the reins are loosened too much, you'll soon slide into debauchery."

So Hoi came to understand that neither the manager nor his coworkers had the luck to see the program he'd watched last night, even though they all hugged their television sets constantly and let themselves be crammed with junk movies like a flock of hens and cocks being fattened with lumps of steamed rice before being sold to the butcher's block.

For the next few nights the programs were very proper, much to his relief. After all, it wouldn't do for parents and their children to sit together enjoying a striptease, would it?

But now he understood what was happening. Only on those evenings when his wife and children were out and he sat alone in the dark bedroom watching television did that program flare onto the screen. And not only that one. There was also a porno film about pigs that contained some truly spectacular sequences. Evidently, these programs were shown only when he was at home alone.

Listening to Hoi's whispered descriptions, his boss Dien was skeptical.

"Really?" He flashed an easy-going grin. "Well, I'd better come over and check it out, see if it's true."

That night Hoi gave his children tickets to the cinema and found an excuse to drive his wife away. As soon as Dien came over, the two men went and sat in front of the television.

The pig film entranced Hoi. But when he turned to Dien to see if his boss liked it, what he saw in his living room was a goat sitting with its forelegs folded on its chest, its hind legs tapping gently with the music. Hoi screamed and rushed to the door.

"What's the matter with you?" the goat asked in a restrained, polite manner, peering at Hoi through its old man's spectacles.

The goat still looked very much like Dien. Around its neck was the gold chain the manager usually wore; an Orient wristwatch still circled its left foreleg. The only difference was the sparse beard on Dien's warty chin, which had been replaced by a pointed goatee, and Dien's clothing, which had been replaced by a thick coat of black-and-white fur.

"Why have you been put into this pitiful condition?" Hoi asked, gradually regaining his calm.

"What do you mean?"

"I mean, you've turned into a goat."

"What? You have the guts to say I've turned into a goat?"

Hoi gave him a mirror. But contrary to his expectations, the goat didn't seem frightened. It gazed at the mirror for a long time and even raised its fore- and hindlegs to examine its hooves. Though the goat seemed to be in silent anguish, it remained unruffled.

"Well, my life is shattered," it sighed, returning the mirror to Hoi. "Never mind, personal affairs must not interfere with the common good. Listen, tomorrow, managers from the construction materials service will visit our factory. As chief of planning, you'll have to welcome them on my behalf. Try to invent a pretext for my absence. . . ."

"I can fabricate something for them, but what can I say to your wife?"

"Don't interrupt. Just tell her I was sent on some urgent business tonight by the ministry and had to catch an early flight south."

"Have you decided to take refuge in my house, sir?"

"Temporarily—just for a few days. Hurry up now, help me find a place to hide."

Hoi had no choice but to lead the goat to the pig shed in the corner of the backyard. Until a short time ago, his wife had brought leftovers from her hotel, saving the choicest courses for the family but giving any stale or spoiled food to the pigs. Lately, the atmosphere at the hotel had become tense, and she no longer dared to bring anything home—and so the shed was empty.

Hoi came home early the next afternoon. Making certain that his wife and children weren't back yet, he approached the pig shed. The goat, under the impression that Hoi would come home to feed it lunch, had been waiting impatiently. When he finally did, the goat could barely keep calm.

"There you are, wasting your time boozing it up with those guys from the construction material service, leaving me here to starve to death!" the goat yelled at him shrilly. "I'm almost done for."

"But what kind of care do you need from me, sir? Isn't the grass on my lawn good to chew?"

"Grass? For me? Are you joking? Get busy and prepare my favorite courses: pullet with lotus seeds, simmered *bain-marie,* chicken chitterlings and pineapple, browned in fat, some fresh bean sprouts, and, if available, a glass of soaked-chameleon whiskey."

"Please—all you need to do is go home and I'm sure your beloved wife will cook those delicious foods." Hoi stuck out his lower lip, pouting, trying to calm down by humming a soft, soothing song to himself. "All right: I'll buy the foods for you, sir. However . . ."

Hoi bent over the pointed ear and whispered that in the meeting today with the construction material service, he'd like to ask for some books, tiles, and cement to be supplied to himself under the pretext of being used for repairs to the factory day care center.

"Impossible!" The goat sprang up onto its hind hooves,

vigorously waving its right fore leg. "That means taking the common property of the people for your individual benefit."

"For whose benefit, sir? Didn't you say that you're hungry?"

"Don't profit from my predicament!"

Hoi left the goat overnight with an empty stomach. Though it was almost too weak from hunger to stand, it didn't dare bleat for help, for fear that Hoi's wife would hear. The goat knew that if it fell into the hands of that gourmet cook, it would end up goat meat, done rare.

The next morning, unable to bear it any longer, the goat accepted Hoi's conditions. Hoi placed some documents he'd already prepared on a pinewood box. The goat took a pen, but sat lost in meditation for a while before it signed. It shook its head in sorrow.

"What humiliation! And just for food."

"Anything we do is just for food, sir."

In no time, Hoi had a heap of renovation materials for his house. Combing through the paperwork, he beat his brains trying to figure out what he could next gain from the goat by forcing it to starve.

He had not yet carried out his plans when one morning Toan, Dien's wife, burst into the house.

"You can fool everybody but me that my husband went to the south—I've just met with the minister, who said my husband had no urgent business he knew about. Obviously, you're an accomplice in some illegal affair he's been having with some bitch."

Sweating heavily, Toan felt Hoi's calmness strike her in the face like a dash of cold water. She saw that beneath his calm was the chilly soul of a cold-blooded killer, and became panic-stricken. But she was also accustomed to being loud-mouthed and arrogant, and whatever was on her mind flowed out uncontrollably.

"Or likely you killed my husband by hacking him into pieces and threw them into the pig shed. Hell, he was wearing his gold chain and watch and his gold-framed glasses."

At the mention of those precious items, her greed and regret at their loss stoked her anger, and she became fearless. She turned and rushed impetuously to the backyard, and to the pig shed.

Hoi had no time to explain or to stop her. Well, let her see, he thought.

At first, Toan couldn't see anything in the dilapidated shed. Finally, after her eyes got used to the dim light, she saw the goat and stared at it for a long time. Suddenly she trembled. "Is that you?" she asked pityingly. "Have you been living in this shed all this time?"

The goat didn't answer. It bowed its head as if admitting fault. Toan noted that the goat still wore the gold chain, the watch, and the gold-framed glasses.

Surprised, Hoi asked her, "How did you recognize him?"

"Why not?" Seeing that Hoi was sympathetic, Toan poured out her heart. "I saw him for the first time like this on the very day he came to ask me to marry him. My parents and siblings were all full of praise for him; he was so handsome and talented, a general manager when he was barely over thirty years old. Only I saw that coming into our house that day was a sharp-bearded goat, insensitive to human beings. But I was a spinster of thirty-three, and he was my last chance. For over twenty years now we've shared our lives, and I always see him as he is at this moment, in this pig shed."

The three were silent for a long while. Finally, Hoi asked, "What are your plans now?"

"Let him stay here—take care of him for a while. I have no place to feed him in my house, and besides, we're having guests from the country. I'll provide food for him, and you'll be paid for your trouble."

"But you'll have to arrange for his return as soon as possible. If my wife discovers the boss," Hoi jerked his chin at the goat, "she'll take him to the Ban Toc hotel and sell him to the Specialized Dish Section."

A few days later Toan brought a jute sack, and they put the goat inside and strapped it to the luggage carrier of her motorbike. Soon the goat was back in his own room, with his own table and favorite books. Toan had carefully prepared a welcome-home party for her husband, including champagne and his favorite foods.

After a glass of whiskey, the goat's eyes grew damp, and his face grave. In a choked voice, he said, "Hitherto, I nurtured a hope. But today it was completely shattered. You two need to start spreading a rumor that after returning from my urgent project, I was so weak I couldn't continue working. And you, my wife, will need to file my application for retirement."

"Why should a goat care about retirement?" Hoi commented carelessly.

"Don't say that. My career, full of satisfaction in every respect, demands a smooth and honorable withdrawal."

"I understand you," his wife nodded. "We'll need to invent a contagious disease for you, so nobody comes to check. All right, I'll tell the Personnel Section of your factory that you have AIDS."

The goat sprang up in anger. "You'll smear my honor and prestige. A Mr. Clean like myself can't fall back on a filthy disease like that as a reason to retire."

After much discussion, Hoi and Toan convinced the goat that he was being treated for hepatitis and pulmonary tuberculosis. Under that pretext they would file the application for his retirement.

Hoi came home tipsy that evening. Nearing the house, he remembered that his two children were away that day, attending a meeting of neighborhood teenagers. His wife would be home alone. He suddenly wondered what kind of program she would watch on his as-you-like-it television.

Hoi glued his eye to the gap between the door and the jamb.

The room was dyed with the pale, sickly light of the television. He strained his eyes for a long time before he was able to make out a figure on the screen: a graceful man displaying his back and chest, spinning like a fashion model. Suddenly, within a second, the model was parading without a stitch on his body.

Hoi banged angrily on the door. He even threw himself against it. His wife quickly opened the door, not even deigning to switch off the television. On the screen Hoi saw the same man, with the same graceful smile, now spinning round and round displaying some new fashions. The change of sequence didn't deceive him.

"Be careful," Hoi scowled at his wife, "I know someone who turned into a goat by watching that kind of film."

His wife calmly returned to her chair.

"People only say that one thing turns into another," she said firmly. "But you're wrong. Nothing turns into itself."

Hoi stood transfixed for a few moments before he caught her meaning.

"You mean human beings are like goats?"

"No, not like. They *are* goats. All I see around me is a society of goats. The houses and the streets are swarming with goats. Goats riding bicycles and Honda motorbikes. Goats sitting in Toyotas."

"Why have you never said this before?"

"Because I would have been thrown immediately into the Bo Dung Mental Hospital. Instead, I greet the male goats as uncles and brothers. And the females as aunts and sisters. Though it's quite different with the flocks of goats delivered each day from the suburbs to my hotel. There I slaughtered one goat, imagining it was the director general of the hotel cooperative, who didn't give me permission to visit France; I also skinned and carved up another that resembled the woman from Personnel who refused to hire my brother. And I prepared special dishes from the meat of that old satyr, the assistant manager."

Hoi shivered. He wanted to ask his wife whether she had always felt she was sharing bed and board with a goat also. But he held his tongue. One always remains happier when one doesn't force another to confirm something they both already understand.

After a time no one remembered the unexpected retirement of Dien due to serious illness. It was said, however, that once a neighbor came in through the open door of the house, looking for Toan. When she didn't see her, she proceeded to Dien's study where she saw a bespectacled goat writing at the table. In front of the goat was a thick pile of paper, with the huge word MEMOIR written in capital letters on the top sheet. Dismayed, she rushed around the neighborhood spewing out what she'd seen until she was finally committed to the Bo Dung Mental Hospital.

As for Hoi's wife, she began bringing home leftover food from work, including Hoi's favorite goat meat. But every day before eating, he carefully read through the obituaries in the newspaper. Only when he was fully confident that Toan hadn't announced her husband's death, only when he was certain she hadn't sold Dien to the Specialized Dishes Section of the Ban Toc hotel—only then could Hoi calmly enjoy his goat meat special.

Translated by Ho Anh Thai
and adapted by Wayne Karlin

A Small Tragedy

Le Minh Khue

ON ASSIGNMENT from the biggest newspaper in town, I went to District V to investigate the murder of a man by his son. The son had killed his father deliberately, according to his confession, and then dragged the body into the back garden, slit open the belly, and pulled out the liver. I did not dare ask him any questions, so I only observed him through the bars of his temporary cell, planning to do a small survey on the increasing crime rate in this region after the war.

Upon my arrival, I received a letter from Uncle Tuyen. He wrote that at the end of the month, my cousin Cay—his oldest daughter—would come up from Ho Chi Minh City with her fiancé, Quang, to visit the family. Taking advantage of new investment laws, Quang returned from abroad to try out a joint shrimp-breeding venture between the municipality and a French company. Quang didn't meet Cay at the office, but at a gathering of some overseas Vietnamese who had returned to work under the investment law, and about twenty intellectuals representing the city. After the conference, people sang and recited poetry, and Quang happened to be an amateur musician and singer. He sang so beautifully that Cay couldn't take her eyes off him. They got to know each other, fell in love, and decided to get married. The children of my father's oldest brother, Uncle Ca, and Cay's brothers and sisters had already moved to Ho Chi Minh City. All of them were young and had made their own way in the world. Some of them had married foreigners, and therefore the love that blossomed between Cay and Quang, who carried a French passport, was nothing unusual. Uncle Tuyen and his wife were reassured because so many of their own children and nephews and nieces had witnessed Quang's introduction to the clan down in Ho Chi Minh City. Now Cay was about to present Quang formally to his future in-laws in the North. After that, Quang would return to France on company business and then bring his mother back here to take charge of the wedding.

I felt bad about my unfinished business in District V. I kept thinking about the man who murdered his father. Outwardly, he looked so normal, even dull. But he had a very pale complexion. Twice I had witnessed a murder in the streets. The killers were neither big nor fierce. Rather, they were pale, cold, delicate, and determined. They could kill without remorse or pity. The man in District V was like that. He seemed content, detached, and extremely cold. His wife had taken off with their child because he had murdered his own father—how could he have any pity on them? People were trying to find out if he was insane. As for him, he seemed indifferent, sitting there behind the metal bars.

But I had to set my work aside and go back. I got a ride with a group of reporters from Hanoi, as they also had to go to the provincial town. This way, I saved a little money and could afford to buy a pretty good present for Cay on the occasion of her engagement. Among Uncle Tuyen's children, I treasured Cay, who was good-natured and beautiful beyond compare. She was born in 1957 and ever since then had lived in a family that received the rationing vouchers reserved for very high-ranking officials. She went to Europe at seventeen to pursue the odd profession of cremation. As stubborn as she was, no one could have swayed her. So she studied abroad for six years.

By convincing those specialists who traveled to Europe on business to take things to his beloved daughter, Uncle Tuyen was able to take such good care of Cay that the young men of France were greatly impressed. In the summer, in her dorm room half a world away, Cay could fill a vase with fresh lotuses from home that had been refrigerated on the plane. Following the specialists' business trips, she could enjoy fresh blood oysters, green water spinach, and fish sauce, and she could even wash her hair with citronella leaves or other herbs. She enjoyed all of these things as if they were as plentiful as the air we breathe. At that time I was also living in a dorm, in Vietnam. I got the lower bunk and developed allergies because of all the dust that fell from the wooden slats on the bed above: my friend in the upper bunk never bothered to dust her bed before going to sleep. During those years, the boys ate their meals in a common kitchen and never used bowls. The rice was tossed into a basin, and then the rest of the food went in, too. With their heads almost touching, the boys leaned over the basin, each with a spoon. The stairways in the dorm were covered with trash and urine. The future intellectuals spent their days at the university gate drinking tea on credit. Their hair was long and unkempt, their complexion pale from malnutrition. There were days when there was no rice at all, and then everyone got only a fistful of boiled flour that was as hard as a rock and a piece of water spinach as long as your arm. I told Cay these stories about my student days, but she seemed indifferent and sometimes smiled. I asked her if she was aware of such things. Of course, she answered, and laughed quietly. I did not know what she was laughing about but I knew she was not indifferent. Perhaps she was thinking: Everything's the same. We have to put up with misfortune as it comes. It's destiny. No one would will such things.

Uncle Tuyen retired three years ago. After that his villa no longer had security guards or other irksome formalities. Now he had his meals with his wife and children, and spent his time watering flowers in the garden or swinging in a hammock tied between two tall shade trees. He had lorded it over his subjects for so many years, enjoying the highest salary and all the best privileges and perks in town. Inside his house, from the paperweight on his desk to the paintings in the living room, from the bookshelf to the doormat, absolutely everything had been furnished by the State, and when he retired they became his own. He had enjoyed everything as if it were the very air that he breathed, so it was inevitable that in retirement he would feel deeply his impotence in the humdrum of everyday life. The life of ordinary citizens was like a dirty, scraggly stranger worming his way into Uncle Tuyen's house. And he could do nothing about it. In the marketplace he was naive. He became angry over the declining purchasing power of the currency, the rudeness of the salesclerks, the fact that "everything had gotten completely screwed up," and so forth. He was like so many of his powerful contemporaries in that he never tried to find out why things had reached this wretched state. Of course, he would vehemently deny that he was one of the people responsible for "screwing things up." He became angry when the authorities put down in his rationing booklet even a kilo of ground pork or the half kilo of butter he wanted for his breakfast. The grocery store that served the high-ranking municipal officials (and which was a big secret tantalizing the university students, who only got vouchers for one-tenth of a kilo of sugar a month) was gradually depriving him and his family of the power to enjoy everything on earth.

The reporters in the car didn't know that I was a niece of Mr. Tuyen. Perhaps they never expected that his niece could be such an impoverished-looking reporter—a reporter who only had a rickety bicycle to toss onto the roof of the car when getting a free ride, a reporter who worked only with a notepad instead of a tape recorder or camera.

From the passenger's seat, the young man with a bucktooth turned around and asked me, "You're a reporter in town. Have you ever interviewed Mr. Tuyen?"

"No!"

"What a pity! I can't understand why you haven't spoken to a man with such a grand reputation."

The man next to me laughed. "He would never have

agreed to meet with you. In his day, he only wanted to meet with, how should I say it, with those who would take a picture of him from the chest up. Because he buttoned all the way up. People were only allowed to see him from the chest up, buttoned to the chin. I wondered sometimes what he wore to bed, and if he ever used the bathroom."

They all laughed. I couldn't. No matter what, Uncle Tuyen was a relative. Dusk was gathering. The car crossed a shallow river. Corn, sweet potatoes, and pumpkins grew on both sides of the river, and there were children chasing each other, filling the air with their laughter. The iron bridge, which was restored after the war, was painted green, contrasting with the sky and water. A long time ago, the bridge was truly majestic, but it was bombed during the war.

The young man with the bucktooth turned around again. "At the start of the war, it was fierce here."

"Really?"

"At that time I was an artillery soldier on the other side of the river, so I know. The F105 planes bombed every day, until there was no fresh air left to breathe. Even so, one day we saw people coming out in droves, thousands. The company commander, who later sacrificed his life in another battle, said the young people were ordered by the chief of the municipal political committee to fill the bomb craters. What? In broad daylight? he'd wondered. Of course! The commander blew a fuse. What a stupid order, he thought. On a sunny day like this, there will be a slaughter. True to his prediction, at 8 A.M. the AD6s were already appearing in the distance. Then the F105s dove down, wave after wave. Our anti-aircraft artillery kept firing. We shot down an AD6."

"And all the people?"

"The vanguard youth? I've never seen so many people die like that. They were empty-handed, puny, running like ants on the naked riverbank where all the trees had already been mowed down by bombs. I tried to dig into one crater to pull out three young girls, but they had died in such a tight embrace I couldn't untangle them. I started sobbing. Later, the old cook somehow pulled them out. They were all city folks. It was nearly dawn before we finished carrying all those bodies away. And the American planes attacked a second time, in the middle of the night."

"What happened to Mr. Tuyen?"

"What?"

"Was he punished for sending those young people out to fill bomb craters in broad daylight?"

"No. Nothing happened to him. There was only a report in the newspapers: 'At the G Bridge we shot down an AD6. The soldiers and people put on a magnificent, heroic struggle. . . .'"

Everyone in the car was silent. Even the driver slowed the car down. Almost twenty years had passed since then. I looked over my shoulder, almost certain that I would see the eyes of the dead, still full of accusation.

After a few moments of silence, the man with the bucktooth said, "Countless people died, and it could have been avoided. It could've been done at night. Why order thousands of people to come out in broad daylight on the open ground?"

"Don't forget that in '76 there was another scandalous event here."

"I know what happened!"

The driver turned to listen. He was in the South at that time, so he didn't know what happened. The man with the bucktooth took his time. "It was Mr. Tuyen again. He was supervising a big project that required manual labor. He threw thousands of young people into the irrigation project. The geology of the area wasn't stable. It was near a limestone mountain and there were pockets of water hidden beneath the ground. The geologists warned him but he wouldn't listen. The drums beat; the flags waved; everyone was full of zeal. The banners and slogans were all bright red. But there was no machinery, and when the ground caved in, there was nothing with which to dig out all the people who were buried."

"How many people died?"

"They didn't report the number. Do you happen to know?"

"No, I don't."

Actually, I knew about that. It was like a small earthquake. A hundred and eighty-six people died. All of them were young.

The man with the bucktooth sighed. "After the cave-in, there was a serious decline in enthusiasm for the project, and it fell down the drain. Who knows how many millions of *dong* were lost? The eye-popping figures were always kept secret."

"In our country things are truly funny: everything is kept secret. In order to protect someone's reputation, everything becomes vague, no one knows what to make of anything."

"Before he retired, he was involved in one more debacle. Or maybe a few more."

"Tell us."

"There's that incident the press have been probing into recently. It happened during the flood season. Tuyen ordered all three counties to dig fish ponds. The young people had to set all their other work aside to go dig those ponds. Then it started to rain. The water began to rise and soon covered all the ponds. That was the end of the fish, and people were exhausted. I heard that some people even died of starvation.

"A foregone conclusion!"

"Do you know about that? You lived here then, didn't you?"

"No. I don't know about it."

"Then you're truly an innocuous reporter. You only write what they tell you to write?"

"Yes!"

I said yes to avoid the subject. There were so many stories like this about Uncle Tuyen. The reporters in our town knew them all but never mentioned them. We were always advised to protect the reputation of our comrade leaders in town.

Night was beginning to fall when our car finally arrived in town. The reporters all went into an inn for a cheap dinner. They insisted that I join them for a little party. The man with the bucktooth looked at me. "Imagine an 'elitist' reporter riding a rickety bike, living in a six-meter-square room, having no boyfriend, looking so serious all the time, acting as if this world were full of important issues. Do you realize this makes you a truly outdated product?"

They all broke into laughter, and I couldn't help laughing, too. The man with the bucktooth kept teasing me. "We ourselves are the losers. We reporters are the fools who keep prying into frivolous matters. And what about Mr. Tuyen? He enjoys all the gifts from heaven, and his children enjoy the leftovers. Only the leftovers, but that's still a life of luxury to us."

I said good-bye to the reporters from the capital and walked the bike along a few narrow streets. All of a sudden, I no longer felt excited. I thought about Cay and had to admit that the man with the bucktooth was right: The children are enjoying the leftovers.

The next morning, I was still in bed when I heard someone knock and call out my name in a voice that was unfamiliar. I jumped up and threw a quick look at my hair in the mirror. The sun streamed through the window. I looked at my face and all the troubles seemed far away. I flung the door open: Cay.

"Hello, little sister!"

Cousin Cay. My heart filled with excitement in the face of her magnificent beauty. She was even more beautiful than before. She had shed her indifference and aloofness. Her passionate eyes locked me in a loving embrace.

"Why didn't you call? I waited so long for you last night!"

"When I got home, I was too exhausted!"

"Something was wrong. Something happened, right? I can tell you weren't too tired to come see me."

I could only smile. Cay was too smart. She was always able to read my mind.

"Can you straighten things up? We have a guest."

"Who?"

"Quang."

"Oh, God! Why did you bring him here? You'll kill me."

"Never mind. I know it'll be okay."

Together we folded the mosquito net and fluffed the pillow. Cay took the broom and gave the floor a quick sweep. During the week that I was away, a thick film of dust had accumulated on everything.

"Go wash your face," Cay said.

I opened the suitcase, pulled out my least tattered shirt, and sprinted to the public bath. How lucky. The water was running. The lights had come on. The sun's rays filled the yard and back alley. I took a bath and went to a neighbor's to comb out my hair. In the mirror I actually looked presentable. When I got back to my room, Quang was already seated inside. His expensive Honda Cub was parked in the front yard. My heart missed a beat when I found Quang sitting on the decrepit chair I'd been using to write my latest sensational stories. The chair was both rickety and rotten from termites. Cay was sitting at the foot of my bed and waved me in.

Quang jumped to his feet, "Cay's told me so much about you. You look just as I expected."

I looked him in the eye. I had never met any man as attractive as he was. I turned to look at Cay and found her smiling sweetly. They were equally attractive, as if they were born for each other. I instantly believed what the physiognomists said, that a husband and wife always have some similar features. Quang looked like Cay in some respects. Their marriage would last. I thought so.

He looked uncritically at all the things in my room, the shabby room of a single girl. Perhaps he had once lived in a room like this, even though, judging by his discreetly simple suit, I could tell that he was wealthy. Those who are rich and take their wealth for granted never show off through their manners or dress. His natural nobility was not something that could be achieved with a university degree. I felt reassured when he sat on my old chair in that room I now no longer felt so ashamed of.

"How's your life going, Thao?"

"You can look and see. This is how I live."

"In France, we have more conveniences, but we don't have things like that, because we have so little time." He was pointing to the landscape *Above the Eternal Tranquillity* on my wall. Every morning I looked at the serenity in that painting and couldn't help shedding a tear before the loftiness of that place where all of us will eventually dwell.

"I bet you often look at it in the mornings."

"Yes."

"Then you cry, right?"

I nodded. We all laughed. What was strange was that I felt a sisterly affection for Quang. He didn't seem like someone from another land. There was something about him that reminded me of my dead brother. That feeling came over me softly, and it was deep. I wanted him to stroke my head or hug me as he would hug his little sister. I hadn't felt so close to anyone for a long time.

After that he pushed the scooter into my room, and we all went out for breakfast. He walked between Cay and me. Even though I met with and talked to countless men every day, I had never met a real man before. In this land, worries about food, the struggle over trivial things, and the mediocrity and insignificance of pleasure had deprived men of their dignity. They had became identical to women. Wherever you went, you only encountered one kind of person and you got so bored you lost the habit of distinguishing between men and women. It had been so long since I had experienced the feeling of walking beside a man.

"Why don't you get married?" Quang asked. "Living like this is so sad."

Cay looked at me out of the corner of her eye.

"There's no one who loves me," I said.

"Because you've never met the right man. Right?"

Cay giggled.

"Sometimes," he said, "that's just a feeling. You must get rid of any hostile feelings. Don't nurture any hostility that isn't necessary. Everything will be fine once you have a lifelong companion."

"It's easier said than done. You have Cay, so you can say that and force everyone to listen. How can I be like you?"

He laughed easily and swung an arm over Cay's shoulder. We walked down a slope to enter the neighborhood where there were restaurants. He grabbed my hand and pulled me out of the way of a car approaching from the opposite direction. I was thrilled. The previous afternoon, in the car coming back from District V, I had pictured Quang quite differently when the man with the buck-tooth mentioned the children of big shots like Uncle Tuyen who enjoyed their parents' leftovers. I imagined Quang with a thin mustache, loosely holding a guitar, singing with a hoarse voice, and eyes half-closed out of arrogance. He would snap his fingers for a cyclo without even bothering to look at the driver, or act cool in public in order to charm the ladies. I don't know why, but I had pictured Quang like a hip singer-songwriter I often saw on TV.

"What dish are we going to treat Quang to?" Cay asked.

"What do you like best?"

"When I was small, I lived in the South; and ever since we moved to France, whenever I eat at home, my mother cooks only southern dishes—sour shrimp with boiled pork, raw vegetables and herbs, crisp fried noodles, ground shrimp barbecued on sugarcane, and soft-shelled crab with sesame rice paper, which we eat while drinking shots of wine.

"Lord, you make my mouth water!"

"I've seldom had a chance to try northern dishes. So treat me to something really delicious, okay?"

"Cay, let's go to fat Mrs. Tu's for *bun thang*."

"Perfect. I haven't eaten that for so long."

Mrs. Tu had a little place at the end of a long alley lined with banyan trees. Even though the shop looked shabby, the noodle dish was beautiful. Mrs. Tu saw Cay and ran outside. "Hello, Miss! I heard you left for the South long ago."

"Yes. I just came back. This is my friend Quang, who's back from France. He wants to try your noodle dish. "I could see Cay's smile in the corners of her eyes.

"The owner's so excited, Quang. She's got a customer from abroad."

Quang smiled rather sadly. "Well, I'm a French national but I'm considered a foreigner in France. And here in Vietnam, even though I have residency, people still think of me as a foreigner."

"Then it's better for you to return to the place where you were born."

"Unfortunately, I don't know where I was born. Of course, I want to come back here. I don't want to live like an exile in France, like an exile in Vietnam, like an exile in the community. I even feel like an exile in my own family sometimes."

It seemed that Quang and Cay had talked about this subject many times. Quang spoke softly, somewhat nostalgically. I didn't quite know what it was all about, so I kept silent, listening to them whisper. Quang turned to me. "I forgot to tell you, Thao. My parents were also northerners, but they both passed away. My adoptive mother brought me to Saigon, and we didn't leave for France until 1970."

"I know all that from Cay's letter."

"After the wedding, we'll live in Saigon."

"What about your adoptive mother?"

"I'll bring her with me. She can't bear to live far away from me. What do you think?"

"I think it's better if you don't come back here to live. This land is full of sadness; how can you put up with it?

Once you're married, I don't think it'll matter greatly if you have to live in France."

"Maybe that's true. This is a photo of my birth mother that my adoptive mother kept for me."

He opened a small wallet and handed me a six-by-nine-inch photo. It was still in good shape even though one could tell that it was taken long ago. I fixed my eyes on the woman in the photo. She had a noble face, beautiful beyond expression. I felt inexplicably moved, maybe because of that lofty portrait. On the back of the picture these words were still legible: "My darling Ti, keep this photo so that you will know your mother. Love Mother Han as you love me. The village of Sam, 1953."

"Why were you called Ti?"

"That was my nickname when I was a kid, because I was born in the year of Ti. In Saigon, my adoptive mother didn't change my name until I was ready to go to school, but at home she continued to call me Ti."

Mrs. Tu carried over a tray containing three bowls of snow-white noodles. Cay followed her, holding a plate of lime slices and chilies. Mrs. Tu said sweetly, "I have a foreign customer and so I prepared the dish myself. It's been a long time since I've done this myself. Usually, I just give orders in the kitchen."

"Please don't call me a foreign customer. I'm one hundred percent Vietnamese."

"But you're a French citizen. You're no longer a Vietnamese. A person like you deserves to carry a French passport. Vietnamese look very dirty. From a life of hardship, you know. You and the young ladies should squeeze some lime juice into your bowls now. Wow, a Frenchman . . ."

I saw that Quang was saddened by Mrs. Tu's enthusiasm. Cay saw it too and cut in. "Tell me the secret recipe for this famous dish of yours."

Mrs. Tu pulled up a chair, sat down, and watched us eat. She smiled brightly. "It's delicious, isn't it? When I do it myself, no one complains. You have to pick a certain kind of castrated rooster, one that weighs at least three kilos. After it's boiled, you have to take it out and use a toothpick to puncture the pocket of water under each wing so that the bird will dry out quickly. That way the meat won't break into small bits when you chop it up."

"What about the broth?"

"It has to be the water the bird was boiled in. Then you put in shrimp, pig bones—it's got to be the knees—chicken bones, mushrooms, fish sauce, MSG, onions deep-fried in chicken fat. . . . It's really an art to do it right, you know. As for the ingredients that go in the bowl, you have to pay attention to both color and scent. Everything has to be both tasty and pleasing to the eye. Thinly cut boiled eggs, shredded sausage, pickled sugar beets, finely ground shrimp, chunks and thin slices of boneless chicken placed right next to each other. Then you also have to put pepper and chili into the fish sauce. Can you recognize all the different ingredients by their smell?"

"This is first-rate. No one in Saigon can make a dish as delicious as yours."

"There are many people who can make this dish, but you have to understand that the spices from other regions don't always go with this kind of noodle soup. They have to come from the North. The flavor that comes from the rice paddy beetles and the herbs of this region are especially delicious. You can't get them anywhere else."

Mrs. Tu sat at our table until we finished eating. She smiled contentedly when Quang finished the last spoonful of broth.

"You really know how to enjoy this dish, not wasting a drop. Leaving even one spoonful would mean not doing justice to the person who made it. Isn't that right?"

She walked with us to the street, insisting that we should all come again. We walked to the embankment by the large river that goes through town. All of a sudden, Cay turned to Quang and asked, "Why don't you try to find the village of Sam?"

"I have to go back to France and ask my mother for more detailed information. She's never told me where the village is. She says no one lives there anymore who would know us. Everybody's dead by now. She seems terrified whenever I mention it.

We stood on the embankment. A breeze blew from the other side. From where we stood we had a good view of the entire town. The port, factories, and strips of marketplaces had begun to prosper over the past year.

"Have you met Uncle Tuyen yet?"

"Not yet."

"Why?"

Cousin Cay leaned her head on Quang's shoulder and said, "He went to Hanoi to fetch his oldest brother, my Uncle Ca. When we got home yesterday morning, he'd just left. Maybe we'll see him this afternoon."

"And you can see I'm getting very nervous, Cay!"

"Relax. He'll like you immediately, you'll see."

"I can't tell how it will be talking to a great statesman."

"No. He used to be a statesman. Now he's only an old man living in retirement, having to start a new life."

We said good-bye to each other after making a plan to meet in the evening. I returned to my empty room and sat listlessly, a prey to sadness and desire. If you're going to love, it should be a big love like Cay's. That's not easy to find, is it?

I rode my bike to the big villa just before the city lights came on.

The entire clan was there that evening. I came in to pay my respects to Uncle Ca. He was eighty years old and had a snow-white mustache and goatee. Long ago he held the position of mandarin or something, and even now he still retained a severe aristocratic air. Uncle Tuyen waved me over. He looked nervous, not as indifferent as he used to be when I came to see him. He asked me about my business in District V. I told him the story of the son who killed his father. He was paying attention to me but following Quang with his eyes.

The living room downstairs was decorated with tapestries from various nations that Uncle Tuyen had visited. A big Persian tapestry depicting an old legend hung in the middle of the room, and it created a festive atmosphere. The tables were arranged end-to-end and covered with a white tablecloth. Uncle Tuyen's wife had ordered all the food for the occasion from the hotel across the street. Two uniformed waitresses had come as well to serve the guests. My aunt wore a long white *ao dai* embroidered with blue flowers. She still possessed the showy habits of a big lady in a small town, which really didn't suit a sixty-year-old woman.

People began to stream into the banquet room. They were all relatives living in town. The old people sat grouped together; the younger ones hurried in and out. Uncle Ca occupied a seat at the middle of the table. Quang came in from the yard, made his way to Uncle Ca, put his hands together, and made a low bow. Then he turned to Uncle Tuyen and made the same low bow, following the ancient ways. Everyone broke into laughter. Uncle Ca seemed to appreciate Quang's gesture. "Why are you laughing? Vietnamese should observe manners like this. For so many years our people were too busy with the revolution to remember these traditions. It takes those who live overseas to cherish them. Treasure it, son."

I sat near them so that I could overhear their conversation clearly. Uncle Ca leaned forward, listening attentively. He always ignored his age, wanting to partake of everything in life. Uncle Tuyen sat across the table, facing his future son-in-law. He was the type who seldom revealed his emotions, but tonight he was deeply agitated. From the moment Quang entered the room, his hands were trembling. I noticed it because he was smoking a pipe and trying to prevent it from shaking. While studying Quang talking with Uncle Ca, his face betrayed a certain deliberation and even some panic. I thought perhaps it was because he loved Cay and wanted to learn more about her fiancé before he could feel assured.

The feast was splendid. I'd hardly ever eaten such dishes before and didn't really know what they were. The room was filled with anticipation. Maybe it was because everyone could sense Cay's happiness. Her beauty shone brightly, and her dark eyes sparkled like pools of water. She looked to the right and to the left and raised her glass to toast one person after another. Quang squinted and cupped his chin in his hand, looking at Cay. This wasn't a

particularly striking posture, so I didn't know why it mes-
merized Uncle Ca. When he looked at Quang, his hand,
grasping a fork with a piece of sausage on it, trembled
ever so slightly. Then he sat back and spent the rest of the
meal deep in thought. Whenever Quang spoke to him,
he only responded with vague nods. He didn't look at
Quang anymore. Instead, he fixed his eyes on a tapestry
from India, which depicted two beloved girls of Krishna
herding cows. I was worried.

When the meal was over, Uncle Ca and Uncle Tuyen
went upstairs to rest. After the older guests had left, one
by one, Quang told us stories about his first days in a foreign land, days of hardship, loneliness, and indignity. He
had to struggle to find a place among strangers, and it
had to be a dignified, decent position, so that no one
would look down on him. Life was so much harder in
France than it had been back home.

While listening to him, I silently leafed through the
pocket-sized photo album that he carried with him.
There were a few photos of pretty young girls smiling by
his side, and the rest were pictures of his adoptive mother.
She was a white-haired woman wearing an *ao dai*. I could
see that, even in an elegant setting, she was still a good-
natured woman of humble origins. In the photos taken
with Quang, she often wore a black dress with flowers
embroidered on its front. There were also pictures of the
yard in front of their small house. A tea table stood in
front of the door, which was covered by a magnificent
blue curtain. Even though they were wealthy, they
seemed to lead a peaceful and simple life. It was a very
beautiful house.

Uncle Tuyen appeared at the window that opened onto

the inside hallway. I was the only one who saw him because Quang was singing and the others were concentrating on his voice. Uncle Tuyen waved to me. I stood up and left the room.

"My wife said that Quang has a picture of his birth mother with him. Is that true?"

"Yes, Uncle."

"Go get it for me."

I returned to the living room. The picture of Quang's birth mother was placed on the first page of the album. I took it and carried it to Uncle Tuyen. He said he wanted to bring it upstairs to take a good look at it. I didn't quite understand, but it worried me.

About half an hour later, Uncle Tuyen came to the window and waved me over again.

"Come upstairs with me. I have something to tell you."

I followed him. He was short of breath, and his body seemed to shrink considerably on the steep stairs inside the house. I asked him, "What's wrong, Uncle?" He made a gesture with his hand as if to tell me, Quiet, and pointed a finger toward the living room where the young people were laughing noisily. By the time we reached his bedroom, he was sweating profusely from his forehead. I hurriedly took out a handkerchief to wipe the perspiration streaming down his face. His forehead was icy. He sat at the foot of the bed, looking like a beggar who had just lost his last few cents to a pickpocket. I almost started to cry.

"What's the matter, Uncle? You're scaring me."

He didn't look at me. Instead, his eyes fixed on the empty wall in front of him. "You're a virtuous girl," he said. "I've always had a lot of affection for you, so I have to let you know. You must stop them at once. Don't let them go any further. Don't let them sleep together."

I panicked. He pointed downstairs. Laughter echoed from below. I understood: "They" were Quang and Cay.

"He's Ti. I abandoned him. God sent him back here to punish me. He's been sleeping with his sister for months already in Saigon. That's how young people live nowadays. They sleep together before they get married. The way they look at each other tells me that they've slept together already. God sent him back to punish me. . . ."

"You're wrong, Uncle!" I sobbed out loud.

"How can I be mistaken? He's the boy named Ti who was born in the village of Sam. His aunt Han took him with her. I know everything. I couldn't do anything at the time. It wasn't my fault. When I first saw him here, I had a premonition. My heart's been throbbing with pain ever since, and I didn't know why. . . ."

He rocked back and forth, talking as if he were in a delirium, as if an excruciating pain were piercing his body. Unable to stop myself, I ran to get Uncle Ca. It turned out that Uncle Ca wasn't sleeping either. He made a motion with his hand: he knew everything already. He followed me to Uncle Tuyen's bedroom. Uncle Tuyen was hugging a pillow tightly. I gave him some water and rubbed some medicated oil onto his hands and feet. I was about to call his wife, but he pulled my arm in panic. "Don't say a word. Don't say a word to anyone. Nobody!"

I nodded.

Uncle Ca said to him, "It's fate, so let it be. What can you do? Send Ti away, and that'll be the end of it. During the meal, it startled me to see the way he sat. He looked just like you when you were a student in Hanoi, as alike as two drops of water. It's fate. We're still rather lucky."

Laughter from downstairs drifted up again. I was horrified. In fact, nothing was really so terrible in a country that had seen only uprootedness, war, and sorrow. I used to think that in old times people just made up the story of "The Stone Woman Waiting for Her Husband's Return." I thought they were wrong to believe that human struggle was futile within the grip of fate and wrong to lament the heartbreaking predicaments of the world. But who would have guessed that such a misfortune could happen to Uncle Tuyen's family? Each era reaps its own tragedies.

My paternal grandfather came from the village of Sam. When he resigned from his mandarin's position at the royal court in Hue, he brought my grandmother, a true girl of Hue, up here to start a new life. When I was growing up, I never heard anyone call it Sam. It was always called March Forward Cooperative—the village of March Forward. Prophecy, the beautiful original name of Sam, had sunk straight down, totally lost in the tidal waves of the revolution. Nowadays, that name only lurked in the memories of old people.

Uncle Tuyen passed the national post–high school exam and got a job with the railroad department. My paternal grandmother married him off to a young lady of the most noble bloodline in town. She was so beautiful that, once she came to live with the family in the countryside, she seldom dared go out. Because of her beauty, none of the tenant farmers could eat or sleep.

My paternal grandfather had passed away long before,

and two years after Uncle Tuyen's marriage, my paternal grandmother also died. The inheritance from an honest mandarin wasn't much—a little land for farming, a tea plantation where they had to hire laborers to harvest, and a compound of tile-roofed houses—but in comparison to the poverty of the countryside at that time, it seemed so big and comfortable that people were jealous. Uncle Tuyen inherited the property because Uncle Ca had followed his daughter to live in Hanoi. My parents also remained in the village. Every day my father went to teach in a town nearby. My mother opened a small tea shop to earn money to send my older brother to school.

After her mother-in-law died, Uncle Tuyen's wife stopped wearing her *ao dai* and bracelets, rolled her hair into a bun, and carried a basket out to the tea plantation. The women were jealous when they saw her: Why is that bitch so beautiful? Why is her skin so fair? She's probably never even had leeches on her feet! The gossip cut into her graceful body. She kept silent and went on with her work in the fields. At that time, it was forbidden to hire anyone to work for you. The tea plantation stretched as far as the eye could see. The work was endless, and at the same time she was pregnant with Ti.

By early 1953, Uncle Tuyen, who had joined the government in the provincial town, could already sense the smell of death in the political atmosphere of the countryside. He wrote a letter telling his wife to wait and not to worry because he would return when peace was established. His wife cried bitterly, because although she was pregnant she had to do all the work. Luckily, my parents were still living nearby.

But no one could do anything once the guerrillas began

to appear every night around my grandfather's house, cocking their triggers and pointing their guns at the people inside the house. And as for Uncle Tuyen, he disappeared into the boiling sea that was politics in those days.

At the end of that year, Tuyen's wife gave birth to Quang, whom she called Ti. When he was only three months old, his mother came down with severe tuberculosis. She was kicked out of the house and forced to live in the rice storage shed at the back of the garden. Fits of coughing exhausted her health. My parents had been separated and therefore weren't able to come and help their wretched sister-in-law. One night my mother did sneak into the garden to bring Tuyen's wife a few handfuls of rice. A hand reached out of the grass, grabbed her foot, and yanked her backward, causing her to tumble into a pile of logs. The rice flew in all directions and disappeared into the grass. My mother was caught and imprisoned in a dark cell for two weeks because they said she was guilty of "making contacts to conceal the property of a landowner." In her desperation, caused by hunger and her child's wailing all night for milk, Tuyen's wife suddenly remembered her cousin Han, a distant relative who was a merchant living alone in town. She sent a message to Han. Han exhausted all her tears begging the authorities for permission to visit her cousin. When they finally met, Tuyen's wife gave Ti to cousin Han. "You must go!" she told her. "Find a way out of here and save his life!"

Tuyen's wife had managed to hide a necklace of pure gold that her parents had given her as dowry when she went to live with her husband's family. Han took the necklace and began to weep. "Oh, Cousin! How can I do it?"

"You must go! Wait until very late, then take the baby on the shortcut to the river and go to the station near the town market. From there, take the baby to Hanoi. Maybe there isn't any trouble there. Then go wherever you can. You have to raise my child for me."

"Oh, cousin! I'm so scared."

"You have to help me. If I weren't so sick I would have escaped already. Keep this photo for him so that he'll know who his mother was. Tell him his father died already. Don't ever let him come back to Sam village. You have to keep him from returning. If he ever comes back, I'm afraid disaster will strike him. Promise me."

"Yes, I promise!"

"The farther you take him from here the better. Don't tell him the way back to Sam village, do you understand? After I die, my spirit will watch over you and your son. From this moment on, you call him your son. . . ."

The moment of departure took place on a rainy night when the cold pierced to the bone. Han took a handful of raw rice and chewed it to a pulp to feed the baby. Tuyen's wife lay on a pile of banana leaves, raised her hand to caress the baby's face, arms, legs, then waved Han away. "Go! Go!"

Han left her cousin some rice she'd brought with her, then disappeared with Ti into the night. Outside, it was cold and rainy, and the guerrillas had abandoned their posts to take refuge inside my grandparents' house. The light from the hurricane lamp shone brightly in the living room and the fits of shouting and laughter enabled baby Ti to slip away quietly. Han carried Ti to Hanoi, then down to Haiphong. She found a way to board a ship headed to Saigon, and thus disappeared from the North.

When Tuyen's wife met my mother, she told her, "I sent Ti away, I can die now." She coughed up blood for a few more days and then died, curled up like a shrimp on her pile of dry banana leaves. My parents were allowed to wrap her in a straw mat and bury her in Con cemetery. Uncle Tuyen never returned, although Uncle Ca had told him that Han had taken the three-month-old baby and that his wife had despised his cowardice and had died a raging death among strangers. He didn't even return to visit the grave of his wife, although he could have done so secretly. He had submerged very carefully, very deeply, and when he resurfaced, he already occupied a very high position. He married a woman from a very safe, simple, peasant background, who became a saleswoman after the land reform campaigns. For many years, Tuyen was of a high-level cadre, answering directly to Hanoi. His position took him all over the world, and his hand signed treaties in many regions. Between these pleasant trips and his great accomplishments were moments of evil, like that bizarre incident in which he sent thousands of young people to their deaths during the American bombing raids. Throughout all those years, Tuyen never lifted a finger to save one single life.

Five months after my mother gave birth to me she died of complications. There was no medicine and no rice. The family couldn't do anything, as they were being watched by the guerrillas. My nine-year-old brother, Toan, sneaked into the fields to steal sweet potatoes and scrounge for grains of leftover rice. My father lay seriously ill in the house. He heard me crying but couldn't do anything to help. At that time, my village was full of

southern recruits for the army. They were poor peasants
in soldiers' uniforms and they hated the children of
landowners as much as the landowners themselves. As
soon as they spotted any children, the soldiers would
jump on them and beat them. The children were so
terrified they didn't dare go outside during the day. The
soldiers came to my house in the morning after my
brother Toan had gone out to look for vegetables. They
surrounded my bedridden father: Down with this son of a
landowner! My father was so terrified by the sound of
their southern accents that as sick as he was he leaped
from the bed and ran out into the yard. Two men used
poles to beat him on the head. He jumped into the pond
where we had once raised lotuses. The two men were so
out of their minds with hatred that they jumped in after
him and beat his head with rocks. They only stopped
when he was dead. My father died with his head in the
water, his brains and blood spread across the surface of
the duckweed-covered pond.

Toan came home and found our father dead and me
wailing and limp from hunger. He was only nine years
old! The sound of our cries was enough to move one kind
soul, an old tenant farmer who used to do housework for
my grandfather. He helped bury my father, then brought
us to his home. Every day the old man gave me one meal
of rice. I was as weak as a wheezing kitten, but I managed
to survive. After some time, the atmosphere of hatred
dissipated, and my aunt returned from town to collect us
and raise us as her own. Toan went into secondary school
when I was still very small. He reached the seventh grade,
then studied pedagogy for three years and became a

teacher. He was a very big and tall young man, but constantly depressed. It was only now, remembering the face of my brother, that I understood why, when I first met Quang, he reminded me of Toan.

One day, during a rectification meeting for teachers in a district near the town, one man wearing white glasses stood at the podium and said sweetly, "Among us there are probably many people who were falsely accused during the land reform campaign. Comrades, please speak up and be frank."

Toan approached the podium and said with passion, "My grandparents contributed rice to feed the soldiers. My father participated in the overthrow of the government in 1945. He was on the district resistance committee. My grandfather's family contributed two revolutionary martyrs. Why was my father beaten to death, and why has the revolution never done anything about it?"

The gentleman in the white glasses gently shook my brother's hand and promised to speak to his superiors.

Toan returned to teaching and two weeks later received a summons to the office of the principal. "You are guilty of being in an immoral relationship with a woman. The educational system needs people of good conduct." The principal thrust an expulsion notice into his face, which bore the signature of the head of school district. Naturally, Uncle Tuyen, as head of the town, must have known about this order, but for a long time his relatives dared not to contact him. He refused to recognize any of them. Now Toan remembered. He was in love with a teacher, Kim, who taught in the same school. She was married. At that time, this was a serious crime, but he

knew that he was being expelled for something more horrendous and that it meant the end for him. He was ordered to return to his birthplace, to return to the village of
March Forward, which was full of awful memories and
peasants who still hated the children of the landowners.
They were afraid that the plots of land that had been distributed to them would be demanded back. Toan came to
our aunt's house to visit me. He held me in his arms and
cried. I insisted that I return to the village with him. He
said, "I'm not returning anywhere. You have to stay here.
You have to study so that you will become an educated
person."

I was still so small, how could I understand his state of
mind? My brother went off in the direction of the train
station and threw himself under the train bound for
Hanoi. My aunt wouldn't let me go near, but I heard people describe the head, the arms, the legs of my brother, all
reduced to a pulp on the tracks. My whole body went
stiff. The feeling of fear overpowered the feeling of love. I
was still too small to understand the meaning of misfortune.

Throughout those years, my Uncle Tuyen lived in a
guarded villa. When Cay grew up, she went off to study
in Europe. Uncle Tuyen allowed her brother Vi to go
study chemistry and then, when Vi returned to the country, arranged a job for him at the municipal planning
committee. The third child, Huong, studied physics and
then worked in the municipal nuclear science institute.
As for the youngest son, Hoang studied automation, and
his father secured a job for him on the price control committee. The professions of the children fit into all the sec-

tors of society, and would never be affected by politics. Tuyen was farsighted in all respects, except for one that he never anticipated: Two of his children, through the vagaries of life, met and fell in love with each other, and were now about to be married.

The next morning Quang and Cay were surprised to see Uncle Tuyen's sunken face. Uncle Ca insisted on returning to Hanoi that morning. Uncle Tuyen motioned to Cay to come closer. "I feel rather tired. Take Uncle Ca to Hanoi and then come back tomorrow. Let Quang stay so I can discuss matters with him."

Quang and Cay held each other as they walked down the stairs. I peeked out the window. They were kissing under the big *muom* tree in the garden. Their kisses were not at all discreet. I thought of the stack of hotel room bills that Cay had in her purse, from an expensive room that they had rented for two weeks. I prayed to the heavens that she wouldn't become pregnant. A child born of this circumstance would probably be missing its arms or legs.

Uncle Ca was packing his things and mumbling to himself while shaking his head. "How miserable! How shameful! Enough! I'm ready to die. What's the point of living longer?" he said to me.

When Cay had gone, Uncle Tuyen said, "Tell Quang to come in here."

Quang was standing with Hoang next to the fence. When he heard me call, he ran up. In the daylight, I was startled: he looked so much like Uncle Tuyen, especially his eyebrows, chin, and lips. Even his large, noble ears had that particular quality that only belonged to people of that lineage. He stroked my head. "The old man is calling me, huh?" I nodded. He hurried upstairs.

I didn't dare to witness the moment when father and son acknowledged each other. I went downstairs to the kitchen to help Uncle Tuyen's wife make spring rolls. Only the family would be eating that day. She was upset because of Uncle Ca's sudden departure. I said, "Old people are as unpredictable as children. Why worry about it?"

Although my aunt was a wise woman, she had no idea that twenty-something years earlier her husband had abandoned a wife and child in a cauldron of boiling oil, abandoned them in a most cruel and brutal way in order to protect himself, like a beast.

She rolled some spring rolls, lifting her hand to brush a lock of hair from her forehead. A pot of soup with ribs in it began to boil so she lifted the lid off, then set it down on the floor. Although she had become a lady, this careless manner of doing things was still in her because she had grown up in the countryside. Somehow she'd managed to acquire a soft and sweet voice—soft as cork, sweet as syrup—and it always sent shivers down my spine. When her husband still held office, she couldn't care less who I was. Despite her own humble origins, once she became a lady she despised the rank and file. She used to follow her husband on all his official visits to wealthy countries. Wherever she went, she greedily cleaned out her hotel rooms of every little luxury from the matchbooks to the bars of soap. She couldn't suppress her greed for trivial things—a mark of people from her background. She was nasty to everyone from her chauffeur to the saleslady in the state grocery store. She was like a servant girl who, once she enters a wealthy house, doesn't remember she's a servant girl anymore. Whenever I looked at her, I was filled with hatred and condemnation. She gave birth to Cay, but I always had a feeling that Cay was actually the daughter of my aunt—the woman who gave birth to Quang.

An hour later I tiptoed upstairs. Uncle Tuyen was lying on his bed as if unconscious. I sprinted down to the garden. Quang was sitting on a stone bench near the fence, smoking a cigarette. I sat next to him. He took my hand silently.

I'd never seen a man as sad as that. I'd only seen despair in the faces of those who had lost their bets in the lottery, in those who were unable to grab one more meter of public housing, in those who were tormented by low wages or lack of food or trivial gossip. . . . I had never seen a face like this, so infinitely melancholic that nothing in the world could lessen his sorrow.

I spoke, and yet I wanted to burst into tears, "So, no one's suspicious. Wait until tomorrow to leave."

"No, I'm leaving this afternoon. Tell everyone, tell Cay, that I had to go suddenly in order to arrange for my mother to come over here, as requested by the old man. You'll also have to invent something, because I'm not going to come back here again. I'm going to abandon the shrimp farming in the South. Cay will think that she met a womanizer. It's better that way."

The atmosphere at lunch was like that of a funeral. Uncle Tuyen was sad. Quang was sad. Who could be happy? Cay's siblings and their girlfriends and boyfriends were all puzzled. Only Tuyen's wife didn't notice a thing. Superficial souls like her prove to be very useful at a moment like that one. She thought that the spring rolls were too salty and that explained why people didn't eat with relish. When Quang said that he had some urgent business and had to catch the Reunification Express at two o'clock, everyone expressed astonishment. He said, "I'll be back in exactly one week!"

From that moment until the end of the meal no one said a word, except for Uncle Tuyen's wife, who kept on chattering. She was the happiest person in the room because she never imagined that anyone could have any trouble. If she hadn't kept chattering, I think everyone else would have cried.

I was in Uncle Tuyen's room when the father and son said good-bye to each other. Quang hugged the stranger who had become his father and sobbed:

"Father! Father, please forgive me!"

"No, it wasn't your fault. Go ahead and go. After a while I'll talk to your sister. Please forgive me."

Both of them began to cry.

The Reunification Express crossed the city and entered the station. Quang stepped into the sleeping car. He looked at me and Cay's siblings through the train window. His face was pale. I sensed that life had left that face already.

The next evening Cay returned home. She wouldn't listen to any explanations. She was even angry with me.

"What do you know? You've never loved anyone so how could you understand? No, don't try to stop me. Why did he leave? We were so deeply in love. . . ."

She caught the Reunification Express that night. Uncle Tuyen became ill. The spacious villa looked empty and even more spacious. I stayed with him a few days but finally had to go back to work. The newspaper asked me to conclude the crime investigation in District V. At that time, articles of this nature were in high demand by the newspapers. It was only necessary for the hawker to yell, "Son kills father and slits open the belly," and the papers would sell like fresh shrimp. I was so sick of it, but it was my work, and I had to do it.

Before returning to the district, I received a telegram from Cay: "Looked everywhere but can't find Quang. Come help me!" How could I go? Not to find him was very lucky.

They had taken the son who killed his father to the municipal police headquarters. I no longer had to travel. He sat at a table on one side of the iron bars; I sat on the other side with my reporter's notebook open in front of me. What I wanted to know was why he had killed his father in such a brutal way. I asked him softly, in a friendly manner, only for the sake of educating young people. He glared at me. He seemed full of hatred, no longer aloof. I took this as a hopeful sign that he might say something, although he still looked pale, gaunt, cold, and ruthless. I waited patiently for a long time. I even smiled at him.

Finally, as if pushed by something inside him, he lurched forward like a beast, baring his teeth and beating his fists against his chest. He growled, "What do you want to know? Why do you want to know? Such an evil person had to be killed. Evil his whole life. Who could bear it? Whatever you want to do with me, go ahead and do it. Slice my flesh and throw it to the dogs. As for him, he was evil, without a conscience; I couldn't live with him."

He kept growling horribly, as if he were out of his mind. Someone had to grab him and drag him back to his cell. I sighed. Another awful history? If I wanted to know, I'd have to search from the very beginning; but the story of Uncle Tuyen's family had left me exhausted.

I returned to my small room. I really needed to go back to that simple place that I now considered my oasis, where there was no one to bother me, and no tragedies. I would have the freedom to enjoy a good sleep, to think by myself, and to gaze at my painting, *Above the Eternal Tranquillity.*

I opened the door and went inside. A telegram had been pushed under the door and was lying on the floor. I opened it and read, "Vu Duc Quang killed himself in the hotel Maxine, fifth floor, room number. . . . The victim asked the hotel staff to inform you. Please come and assist us in our inquiries."

Perhaps it had to end that way. But I couldn't bear to think of my cousin's handsome face fading away, slowly decomposing in the black earth.

Translated by Bac Hoai Tran and Dana Sachs

Crossing the River

Nguyen Huy Thiep

GETTING ONTO the ferry were a monk, a poet, a teacher, two antique dealers, a mother and child, two young lovers, and the ferrywoman.

The ferrywoman laid down a plank so that the two antique dealers could push their motorbike onto the ferry. One of the dealers, a tall skinny guy, said to the guy in the checkered shirt, "Careful!"

He was telling his friend to be careful with the bundle of fabric in his arms. There was an antique pot inside it.

"Help!" The tall skinny guy called to the man behind him. That man was the poet.

They busied themselves pushing the motorbike onto the plank. The poet tilted the motorbike over on its side. He then fell on his knees in the water.

The couple on the shore burst out laughing. The girl said to her lover, "Give them a hand!" The young man took his jacket off and gave it to the girl. He went to the place where the motorbike had fallen.

The motorbike was raised and pulled onto the ferry next to the mother and her child, who were traveling back from the city to visit their home village. The woman was thirty-two years old, beautiful and aristocratic. Her son was nine and looked very cute.

The motorbike tipped over in the ferry's hold, bumping the woman. She frowned. The tall skinny guy quickly said, "Sorry, lady." The tall skinny guy bent down, brushing the dirty spot off the woman's knee. She pushed his hand off, and turned her face away. Behind them, the monk was telling the teacher a story about Bodhidharma.

"One day when the Venerable Master was sitting in the Jade Temple at Tung Son, Hue Kha came to him, cut his hand, and asked for spiritual guidance. He said, 'Venerable Master, my mind is not at peace.' The Venerable Master said, 'Show me your mind.' Hue Kha replied: 'Teacher, I have searched for peace of mind unceasingly, and yet I can't find it.' The Venerable Master said, 'There! I've set your mind at peace already.' Then Hue Kha found enlightenment. . . ."

The guy in the checkered shirt, holding the bundle of fabric next to his belly, sat down in the center of the ferry next to the monk. This was the safest place in the boat. The teacher was not pleased.

"Hey! Why are you elbowing your way in here?"

The guy in the checkered shirt was bashful. "Please forgive me, Grandfather. I'm carrying a precious treasure in my arms. If this pot breaks, I'm ruined."

"What kind of pot?"

The guy in the checkered shirt shrank a bit and said nothing.

The couple got onto the ferry. They sat down in the front, behind the ferrywoman. The young man put his hand out to grab the jacket on the girl's thigh. His hand touched the warm flesh of her belly. He was quiet, and he didn't pull his hand out again. The girl blushed and put the jacket over his hand.

The poet sat unsteadily on the edge of the ferry. He dipped his hand into the water, making the ferry tip. The tall skinny guy scowled and tapped the poet's shoulder. "Don't fool around! We all may die if you do that."

"The water is so transparent!" the poet said. He was astonished. "Look at the fairy fish down there."

The tall skinny guy burst out laughing, "Really? I only see perch."

The boy interrupted, siding with the poet, "They are fairy fish!"

The tall skinny guy glanced at the woman's belly. "Hey kid, ask your mother whether those are perch or fairy fish."

The woman grew embarrassed, drew her thighs together, and jerked the boy's hand.

The ferrywoman pushed off on the pole. The ferry moved away from the wharf. It was late afternoon; the sky above was gray. A bird flew toward the mountain. The ferry tilted to one side.

"Ferry!" A sharp cry rose from the shore.

The tall skinny guy waved it away. "Ignore it!"

The ferrywoman hesitated.

"Ferry!" This time the cry was sharper. The ferry turned and headed back to shore.

Descending the bank was a big, tall guy with a bag draped over one shoulder. He had a look of wind and dust. In one leap he was inside the ferry. River water splashed all over the monk.

"Buddha save me!" the monk cried, startled.

The teacher grumbled. "Man or devil! He looks like a robber."

The guy was in fact a robber. He smiled politely as if to apologize to everyone and then calmly picked up an oar. Hanging his cloth bag over one end of the oar, he tucked it under his armpit to light a cigarette, then gave the ferrywoman a wink. "It isn't sunny. It isn't rainy. It's late afternoon already."

The ferrywoman responded aimlessly, "There's no storm, so why is the raven coming down off the mountain?"

The robber said cheerfully, "I've been invited to a wedding. A sixty-year-old man is marrying a seventeen-year-old girl."

Everyone on the ferry was completely silent. Nobody was fond of this kind of talk. Only the lovers weren't paying any attention. The young man slipped four fingers through the elastic of the girl's trousers. The girl would have made some gesture of resistance but, fearing everyone would notice, she sat still.

The sound of the oars in the water was very soft. The guy in the checkered shirt dozed.

The teacher continued his conversation with the monk. "Oh, venerable bonze! The nature of human life is cruelty. People run after sexual passion, money, and vainglory."

The monk looked into the palm of his hand.

"Oh, venerable bonze! I see beasts everywhere. Everything is a beast. Even faithfulness is a beast. Even the sense of goodness is a beast, too."

The poet recited softly, "Only myself, lonely among the crowd. . . ."

The mother peeled an orange and handed it to her son. The boy shook his head.

The tall skinny guy pulled out a pack of cigarettes and offered it to the poet. The poet noticed a beauty mark on the guy's nose. He shook his head. "What a frightening beauty mark!"

The tall skinny guy glared. "Why is that?"

"You could suddenly just kill somebody." The poet gestured as if to slit his own neck. "Just like that. . . ."

The tall skinny guy burst out laughing. "How do you know?"

The poet stammered, no longer sure of what he was saying. "I'm a prophet of the future."

The boy pulled at his hand. "Then what about me, Uncle?"

The poet looked with concentration into the boy's eyes and saw, together with those tiny red veins, an anxious and numb sadness that the boy seemed to have inherited from his ancestors. He asked gently, "Do you dare to dream?"

The boy nodded resolutely. "Yes!"

The poet smiled. "Then you are unlucky."

The woman sighed.

The teacher grumbled, "There are liars everywhere."

The girl sitting in the front of the ferry stirred. Her lover slipped his four fingers a bit deeper into her underpants. The gesture did not slip past the eyes of the woman. Through her own female experience, the woman knew that the lovers were getting into monkey business.

The teacher recited:

Heels muddied in the pursuit of wealth and fame,
Weather-beaten faces revealing life's cataclysms,
Thoughts of helping the world bring pain.
Bubbles in the ocean of misery, duckweed at the dark shore's
*   edge,*
The taste of the world's troubles numbs the tongue,
*   fills the body with misery.*
The journey through this world is bruising, full of obstacles.
Waves in the mouth of the river rise and fall.
The boat of illusion pitches and rolls at the edge of the
*   waterfall . . ."*

The poet exclaimed softly, "How interesting! Whose poem is that?"

The teacher answered, "That's Nguyen Gia Thieu."

The poet sighed, "What a pity. The interesting ones die. Literature always dies so young. . . ."

The girl at the front of the ferry moaned. The woman looked deeply into the girl's eyes and cursed under her breath, "Wanton!"

The girl heard the curse and turned her face away, but she was still followed by the woman's gaze. Unable to bear it, she shamelessly looked directly into the woman's eyes and admitted, "Okay, I'm a wanton!"

The boy burst out laughing because he saw a drop of saliva running out of the corner of the mouth of the antique dealer in the checkered shirt.

His eyes were shut, and the top of his head pressed against the face of the monk. The fabric bundle in the hand of the guy in the checkered shirt was resting on the teacher's thigh. The teacher was irritated and snatched the bundle, causing the cord securing it to slip and expose the pot. The guy in the checkered shirt woke up, startled. "I'm sorry, Grandfather!"

The teacher lifted the pot to admire it closely. "This pot is so beautiful!" and turned to the monk at his side. "Oh, venerable bonze! Which period does this pot belong to?"

The monk looked up. In his eyes there was a gleam of light, like a ray of desire. "It's a ceramic pot from the time of the Northern domination, the time of Ly Bi or Khuc Thua Du. . . ." Hesitating for a moment, the monk lifted his hand to touch the mouth of the pot. "If Tuong Pagoda had a pot like this and sold it, the money would be enough to rebuild the three gates."

"Then, there's $500 there!"

The tall skinny guy proudly took the pot from the hand of the teacher. The robber stopped rowing. Nothing on the boat escaped his notice.

The girl sitting at the front of the ferry turned away to avoid an impetuous and careless gesture from her lover. The irritated young man pulled his fingers out of the girl. He stealthily wiped his hand on the boat's bottom plank, but he could not scrape one sticky, curly hair off his finger. At that moment, an idea occurred to him which made him suddenly angry. He moved far away from the girl: "Women . . . devils . . . completely worthless . . . dirty. . . ."

The girl stretched out her legs. Her look of hopelessness caught the woman's attention. The woman smiled, unable to hide the look of satisfaction in her eyes.

The poet examined the pot with admiration. "Thousands of years of history. It's really amazing! In the past, a princess used this pot to store shampoo!"

The tall skinny guy smiled. "I thought it contained alcohol."

The poet nodded. "That's right! In the thirteenth century when the Mongolian army came through, a soldier used this pot to hold alcohol. It was buried in the fifteenth century."

"Really?" The tall skinny guy was interested. "There are probably many legends about this pot, don't you think?"

The poet nodded firmly. "Naturally." He narrowed his eyes. "There are fifty legends about it."

The teacher dropped his bag from his hand. The guy in the checkered shirt stooped to pick up a piece of paper and saw that it had words written on it. He glanced at it and read, "'Humanity has a duty to work without stopping to create lofty people: That's humanity's mission and there's nothing else.'—Nietzsche. 'I often speak with artists—and I'll speak forever—the ultimate goal of all conflicts in the universe and among human beings is drama, because conflict serves no other purpose.'—Goethe."

The guy in the checkered shirt returned the paper to the teacher. He said politely, "Your handwriting is so beautiful!"

The teacher took the paper and said bitterly, "Handwriting? What's the point of good literature and beautiful handwriting?"

The boy leaned into the body of the poet. The boy

thrust his hand into the mouth of the pot. The woman panicked, "Son! Be careful! If you can't get your hand out there'll be trouble!"

Maybe the exhortations of the woman were really the curses of the Creator, leveling all the punishments of the past.

The tall skinny guy jumped. "Pull your hand out!"

The poet joked, "When you put your hand into history it'll be stuck there for a long time!"

The boy struggled. It seemed as if the mouth of the pot got smaller the more he moved. "Mama! Help me!" he cried.

Everybody in the ferry jumped. The boy couldn't get his hand out of the mouth of the pot.

The woman was frightened. "What will we do?"

The guy in the checkered shirt sat down to help hold on to the pot. He turned the pot and grumbled, "You devil! You're unspeakably bad!"

The boy burst into tears. The tall skinny guy began to get angry. The robber didn't row anymore. He moved closer to investigate. "Jerk your hand out!" he advised the boy.

The tall skinny guy grimaced and said harshly, "Be careful not to break the pot!"

There was only a little way to go before the ferry reached shore. The river was as calm as a sheet. Blue smoke rose from a far-off village.

The young lovers also abandoned their seats and moved closer to the boy. Everyone searched for a way to disengage the pot. Tears filled the boy's eyes.

The poet joked, insensitive to the scene, "All you have to do is cut off the boy's hand to save the pot, or break the pot to save the boy's hand."

The woman wept and groaned, "Oh, God! I'm so miserable!"

The tall skinny guy held on to the pot. He jerked hard. That was the final effort. The boy's wrist got red and scratched.

"Impossible!" the tall skinny guy said. He stood up and thrust his hand inside his shirt. The guy in the checkered shirt understood his friend's idea.

The ferry reached the dock. There wasn't a soul in sight on shore.

A cold wind blew.

The tall skinny guy and the guy in the checkered shirt drew two sharp daggers. The tall skinny guy said to the woman, coldly and precisely: "This pot's worth about $500. You solve it!"

The woman was frightened and held the boy tightly. "Oh, God! I didn't bring any money. . . ." Suddenly she remembered something and hurried to pull a ring off her finger.

The tall skinny guy turned his head toward the guy in the checkered shirt, who immediately took the ring and put it into his shirt pocket.

The tall skinny guy pressed his dagger into the boy's neck. A drop of blood flowed out on the tip of the knife. The drop of blood ran slowly out of a white streak in the child's skin.

"Why do that?"

The teacher shivered and dropped his glasses. The tip of the dagger pressed deeper. A small spray of blood spurted out onto the teacher's hand.

The girl standing next to the young man covered her face and screamed. She fell against the side of the boat. The young man pushed the poet out of the way, pulled a ring off his hand, and offered it to the guy in the checkered shirt. He said, as if it were an order, "Let the boy go!"

The woman stopped crying. She was rather surprised by the young man's behavior. The tall skinny guy turned his eyes. The dagger's tip sunk deeper into the neck of the boy. The guy in the checkered shirt took the ring out of the young man's hand.

The robber pushed his way through, trampling the boy's foot. The boy screamed. The robber leaned in, pushing against the teacher. The fabric bag hanging on his shoulder fell off, spilling out the tools of a profession that was clearly not at all honest: A fighting stick, as many as fifty different types of keys, a bayonet, a pair of figure-eight curved handcuffs, a crushed and tattered yellowed calendar foretelling the good and bad days.

The robber hurriedly stuffed his tools back into his bag. He held up the fighting stick and tapped it in his hand. He said, "It happened already. Take it as bad luck. A lost investment!"

The tall skinny guy glared up at him. The robber was half joking, half serious. "Stop it! Children are the future! Whatever you do, it has to be humane."

The tall skinny guy hesitated, easing the tip of the dagger. At that moment, the stick in the robber's hand struck the mouth of the pot.

The ceramic pot shattered.

The poet let out his breath and said appreciatively, "That did it!"

The boy collapsed onto his mother. The mother and child held each other, crying. The tall skinny guy and the guy in the checkered shirt were speechless. They turned and pointed their daggers in the direction of the robber.

The robber stepped back little by little then jumped onto the shore. He rotated the stick in his hand.

"It's useless," he said calmly.

It really was useless. Obviously.

The young man helped the girl get up. The girl smiled. She knew she would love him forever.

The poet mumbled, "Love makes people noble."

The two antique dealers put their daggers away, then pushed their motorbike up onto the shore. They grumbled and cursed until they got on.

The teacher was stunned. What had happened amazed him. "Heavens! He dared to break the pot! What a hero! A revolutionary! A reformer!"

The ferrywoman hid a smile. She knew the misfortune of anyone who happened to meet that man alone at night.

The poet picked up a few ceramic pieces and gave them to the woman. "A souvenir," he explained.

He bent down to lift up the boy. One by one everyone went up to the shore.

Dusk was gathering. The monk remained motionless inside the ferry.

The ferrywoman said cautiously, "Venerable bonze! Please go on up to the shore."

The monk shook his head. "No, I've thought about it.

. . . Take me back." Vacillating a second longer, he said, "I'll go later."

The ferrywoman looked at the stars at the edge of the sky. "Venerable bonze, after returning to the other side of the river, I don't come back again."

The monk was cheerful. "It doesn't matter. One can go if one wants. In the past, the virtuous Bodhidharma crossed the river on a stem of grass."

The ferry returned to the wharf. The shadows of the ferrywoman and the monk were clear on the peaceful river. The moon rose, and a bell sounded sweetly.

The monk whispered the invocation, *Gate gate! Para gate! Para para samgate. Bodhi svaha!**

*Translated by Dana Sachs and Nguyen Nguyet Cam
(with special thanks to Bac Hoai Tran)*

---

*A Sanskrit line from *The Heart Sutra*: "Going. Going. Thoroughly Gone. Awakened!" Mahayana Buddhism has functioned in Vietnam for nearly two thousand years. *Paramita*, the Buddhist term for perfection, means literally "to get to the other side." Bodhidharma brought *dhyana* (Japanese: Zen) Buddhism from India in the fifth century A.D.

The Stranded Fish

Doan Quoc Sy

Long ago there was a young soldier:

> *Wearing a conical hat,*
> *Yellow bag over his back,*
> *Long gun on his shoulder,*
> *His hands grasp rifle and lance.*
> *When the order comes*
> *He steps up to the boat,*
> *The drums thunder;*
> *He steps down into the boat,*
> *Tears wetting his face like rain.*

The trip up the river lasted several days. Then the passengers were told to disembark and take the land route. They crossed streams, climbed mountains, took to other boats, then again, leaving these, marched through the jungle. One month had passed before they reached their isolated garrison. This was at the frontier where day and night the sounds of rushing cataracts could be heard; where the mountains were high and forbidding, one peak succeeding another endlessly, barring the way home. Along both banks of the swift river were dark, ancient forests infested with poisonous snakes and wild beasts.

Poor soldier . . . he was so young and yet he had to stay here for three years. Three long years to worry and yearn for home. Any day something might happen, and he would die in these grandiose but cruel surroundings. If he went down, a small leaf would be enough to cover his body, for well before the leaf rotted away his body would disintegrate and disappear into the humid black mud, the underside of the jungle.

At night when the young soldier slept, such images rushed back with the roar of the cataracts and filled him with fear. Three years . . . three long years . . .

> *Three years of garrison life,*
> *On guard at dawn, paperwork at night.*
> *Trees are cut and sawed into lumber:*
> *It was Fate, so why complain?*
> *For food only bamboo shoots,*
> *For friends, only bamboo trees.*
> *In the clear blue water a little fish*
> *Delightful and free . . .*

One day, while looking for lumber, the young soldier lost his way and chanced upon an area round and deep, crowded with rocks—boulders, stones, and pebbles as small as gravel. The water was crystal clear, and in it he saw a little fish. Quickly the fish darted around and tried to take cover. But the homesick young soldier was only thinking of his own wish to be free. So he sang:

> *In the clear blue water, a little fish*
> *Delightful and free . . .*

Strangely enough the fish replied, asking the soldier, "You think I'm very happy in here, don't you?"

"Yes," answered the young soldier, "I do. You must be very happy in there. It's so peaceful, and the water's so clear. You're all by yourself . . . leisurely, free. . . ."

The fish pretended to laugh ironically, then continued, "There used to be a beautiful stream here. One day it rained and rained and rocks rolled down from the mountain, damming up the current. The old stream changed its course and left this dead portion here. At first, when the water was still quite muddied, I felt all right. I swam around and ate plenty, paying attention to no one; and no one knew I was here. But slowly the water became clearer and clearer. By the time only one moon had gone by, the water became as clear as crystal, and I felt so ashamed. It's not only unfortunate to get caught in a dead stream, but to be stranded in such clear water, that's very sad and very degrading."

"If the water's clear, there's not much to eat. Have you been going hungry?" asked the young soldier.

"I can eat the moss off these rocks."

Taking a rice ball out of his bag the soldier said, "Shall I break this into small pieces for you?"

The voice of the fish was tranquil, but sad. "Thank you very much. If only the water were muddied . . . but it's so clear you could see me swimming about snapping up your rice. What a humiliation! What a humiliation!"

The young soldier stood in silence for a moment, then seemed to recall something. "Say, my friend, why not let me take you out of this place and carry you over to the river nearby?"

The fish replied, "Thanks, really. But you see, if I let you take me in your hand that's ten thousand times more degrading than if I remain here in this dead stream. Though I remain here, day and night I can hear the river and feel its tremor through the veins of the earth. One day I'm sure . . . I'm sure a great mountain rainfall will make this hole overflow and flood that stream, and then I will follow the current to the great river. That will be beautiful . . . that will be beautiful!"

Sounds of the evening drum reverberated through the jungle, calling the soldiers to their barracks. Regretfully the young soldier bade the fish farewell.

From then on, whenever he was in the jungle, he tried to keep away from the dead portion of the old stream so as not to disturb the fish in its captivity and solitude. Once or twice, when the mountain rains came down very hard, he would run to the dead stream and throw a handful of rice into the muddied water. But the young soldier's heart was not at peace for he could not help wondering if the fish was still there to receive his gift, or if it had already wriggled over the rocks and found the great river of its dream. . . .

Translated by Vo–Dinh Mai

A River's Mystery

Bao Ninh

RIVERS, LIKE TIME, flow without stopping. Like time, they bear witness to many happenings. This is true especially at night when the river that winds through my village sparkles with thousands of mysterious luminous points. Among them lies the secret story of my life.

At the height of the heaviest flooding that particular year, a wave of American war planes destroyed a levee near my village. After the roaring of the jet engines and the horrendous exploding of bombs, the river thundered through the levee and crashed down onto the rice fields.

From the watchtower I dashed desperately toward the village. That afternoon, my wife had gone into labor, but, dutybound, I had been unable to leave my post. Now, with the sky caving in, my mind could think of nothing but my wife and my new baby. I ran at top speed, the great flood at my heels.

The village was completely submerged in water. I had just managed to get my family up to our roof when a second tide swept in. In an instant, the thatched roof was spirited away into the dark night. Luckily, it got caught up in the branches of a banyan tree where it sat precariously suspended as the tide threatened to rip it to shreds.

A crowd of villagers was also clinging to the limbs of the big tree. Several hands reached down to pull us up. My wife held fast to her newborn, refusing to hand it to me.

"It's a boy, darling!" she cried. "It's a boy! Don't worry about me! I'll hold on to him. You know how clumsy you are, my dear."

The storm raged for several more hours. The river stopped rising, but its current remained strong. More people landed in our tree, which began to look like an overloaded boat running aground. It was a very dangerous situation. With one hand holding the tree and the other clutching my wife tightly, I grew overcome by exhaustion. My wife seemed weaker and weaker; her body was drenched and cold, but she still tried to keep the baby from getting wet.

Toward dawn, I heard a sudden thud below the tree, followed by the cry of a woman choking on water.

"Help us!" she cried. "Help my baby and me! Oh, heavens!"

A frozen hand thrust upward to catch mine but descended before I could grab it. Startled, I bent down, trying to seize it but not in time. The branch we were hanging on to began to shake violently. Frightened and nervous, my wife lost her grip. *Plop!* Our baby, whom I had still not been able to see, slipped out of the plastic bag where he lay in his mother's arm and into the dark torrents of the flood.

"Oh, God! My baby . . ." my wife screamed and plunged down into the water.

I dove after her. The water was cold, murky, deep, and

flowing rapidly. Flailing around desperately, my hands came across the baby. I surfaced and handed it to the outstretched hands above. I then dived back into the current to search for my wife. Several people jumped down to help me.

When I awoke, dawn had broken and it had stopped raining. I found myself lying in a canoe packed with flood victims. Tears came to my eyes. The night before I had been under water for hours searching in vain for my wife. My nose and my ears oozed blood. When a military boat came to rescue us, they had to drag me from the river. I passed out from exhaustion and grief. When I came to, the women in the boat came over to comfort me.

"Since your wife couldn't escape her fate, please take care of yourself so you can live and look after your baby. It's a miracle that you found it before it was too late. To think that a newborn survived such a terrible ordeal! It's one tough baby. Look, it's been fed and is asleep as if nothing happened."

The woman who was comforting me unwrapped my child and changed its diaper. What I saw there left me stunned and speechless. The baby was a girl! I had saved the baby of the woman who had cried for help last night. As for my son, he was with his mother in the cold, pitch-dark abyss.

"My baby!" I burst into tears like a child, holding out my hands to receive the bundle from the woman. "Oh, my baby!"

Since then much time and water have flowed by. I am now advanced in age, and my daughter has become the most beautiful girl in the village. Everybody calls her the child of the river because they all know that she fell into the stream, and that I rescued her. But apart from the river and me, nobody, including my daughter, knows her real story.

Every now and then I go up onto the levee and watch the river. My wife, my son, and the nameless woman seem to be looking up at me from the bottom of the river. Months and years have passed. The river and history have changed. But I have never recovered from my pain. Words are inadequate to describe it.

Translated by Tran Qui Phiet

The Color of Sorrow

Nguyen Qui Duc

SHE HAD FEET to die for. I was back to thinking about them.

"I can't believe you two," Tuan said.

I knew that was coming. We had been silent, taking our time with the bowls of noodle. The heat of the day had cooled off. The occasional breeze was helpful, it made the pollution bearable, and I wasn't sweating so badly. "Believe what?" I said and started to wave my hands under the table. The place was full of mosquitoes.

"I went to the bathroom, came out, and you guys were in love," Tuan was saying.

I drank the last of my Tiger beer. "*Tao dang yeu a*? I'm in love?"

"You're asking me? Maybe she went for your rogue pretensions. Your five-day growth and all that. So, you going to marry her? Bring her to the States?"

I lit a cigarette. Tuan was lighting one of his Marlboro Lights. "She's got a husband," I said. "He's bringing her. Anyway, marriage is a leading cause of divorce."

"For sure," Tuan said. "Not even six months, I give them. What're you gonna do? Wait 'til then? Think you'll get serious?"

Tuan was struggling. We'd been friends for twenty-some-odd years. He could always see my side. But he also knew the guy she married. I slapped my hands together, caught a mosquito. "I'm not waiting for anything, man," I said.

"What're you seeing her tomorrow for then?"

"You jealous or something?"

"Minh, you're pissing me off. What am I going to tell the guy?"

"I'm just seeing her," I said. "For breakfast. She's taking me to some bookstores." I threw my cigarette down the gutter. "Man, I smoke way too much here."

"Me too," Tuan echoed. "Me too."

"I don't know what I'm doing with her," I said. "I've got four days left here. D'you have to tell her husband anything? Isn't he bad news anyway?"

"No," Tuan said. "Just a dork, I guess. She has no idea. I just know it, they're not going to last."

"Damn. Damn!" I said. "Damn mosquitoes. Should we go?"

"Yeah, let's go. Think you can get the engine to start?"

We left a bunch of money on the table. The owner of the noodle stand got up from her aluminum chair. "Thank you, brothers," she said. "Come back again."

The scooter engine started fine. You could hear it fine, roaring in the dead of the night. "Now the lights won't work," I said as we rode off. It must have been 1:00 A.M. The whole town seemed asleep. I started worrying about being out this late. It might be okay for people in town, the locals. But us two, riding without lights. I didn't have my passport on me or any other papers. What good would my driver's license do anyway? It was from California. It actually was chilly, riding like that in the wind. Maybe it was the darkness. "There's no lights anywhere in this town," I said.

"Used to be," Tuan said from behind me. "Saigon was always lit up at night."

"Wasn't there a curfew then?"

"We'd be out late anyway," Tuan said. He tapped on my shoulder. "Turn left here."

"I can't see shit," I said, but turned anyway. Tuan guided me toward his mini-hotel at the end of an alley. It smelled bad. We forgot about the curfew and the war of twenty years before. We had gone to high school up in Dalat, and we were good friends; then Tuan moved to Saigon. When the war was over, we ended up in Los Angeles. Tuan was the one friend I had who didn't become an engineer, a computer scientist, or an accountant. It was great that we'd returned to visit Vietnam at the same time.

"See you tomorrow," Tuan said and got off my bike. "Call me or something."

"Yeah, I'll call you or something."

"Let me know what happens."

"Nothing's going to happen." I turned the bike around. I took off alone. It was cold, and dark, and I was a bit fearful, and drunk. But I was thinking of her face, of breakfast, and it felt good. I was missing her already.

I wasn't intending to get involved with anyone when I left California. I had a research project and a deadline. So I flew back to Vietnam. Wasn't looking for anything. Not love. Or marriage.

By the time the airplane landed, it was close to midnight. I was exhausted and could not tell what emotions coursed through my veins. But it felt a little sad and strange to hear a Korean pilot greet me in accented English. *Welcome to Vetta-Narm*, he announced. *The tempitur in Ho Chi Minh is cullenly 87 dagleez*. He, too, was tired. Too tired to say the name of the city in full. Ho Chi Minh City was just Ho Chi Minh. Out of habit, I preferred the original version, Saigon.

The pilot was silent now. We'd arrived at the end of the line. There were no connecting flights to announce. Or precautionary reminders. When the airplane was rolling, one could stand up, withdraw one's bags from the overhead bins, or walk along the aisle to the bathroom.

I unfastened my seat belt, stuck an unlit cigarette between my lips, peered out. There was no light outside. Darkness separated me from Saigon. Its people were asleep, leaving blackness to welcome me home. I resented it. What can an absence of light at the point of arrival announce other than the poverty and misery of a place? I was prepared to learn about Vietnam's postwar problems, but complete darkness outside my airplane window was a reminder of all the sorrowful things Vietnam has had to carry in its soul through the years of warfare and beyond.

When the war in Vietnam ended in 1975, I joined the Vietnamese who went to America to take refuge. We added our names and ethnicity to the lists of people who have abandoned ancient worlds to come renew the American dream and youthful spirit. I carried on with an American life: a car, an apartment, college, work, credit cards, friends, etc. I also clutched close to my heart the exile's belief that it would be possible to live again in the land where my umbilical cord is buried. As the years went by, the idea of going back to Vietnam became a drug I needed to confront or I could not rest. So I flew across the Pacific. Saw again my childhood home, my old school, relatives and friends. The renewals were fraught with guilt but full of tender emotions, too. The Vietcong became real people. Flawed and damaged by communism, but no longer the monsters that had once terrorized the southern half of the country.

I walked off the Korean airliner into the darkness and the heat of the Saigon night. Tried to ignore the sweat collecting under my shirt, but all I could do was stand back from the passengers fighting for a seat on the bus to the terminal. No one talked. No one smiled.

I had a smoke, but it wasn't like I could be at ease standing in line at the immigration counter. Vietnam was having trouble welcoming back its sons and daughters from overseas, the *Viet-Kieu*s. They have skills and money, but also ideas and attitudes. The immigration officer didn't smile once. Absolutely stone-faced, he shuffled through the pages of my passport. Like it was some kind of dirty magazine. Studied the stamps from my other trips.

"Business?" He didn't even look up.

I shook my head. Said a slight no.

"What're you doing here? Girlfriend? Getting married?"

I smiled, but he still wasn't looking up. "No, no. Research."

"Sure," he said.

By this time, the $10 bill between the pages of my passport had disappeared. Fingers faster than a cobra's tongue, Mr. Stone-Face.

I took a taxi to a hotel downtown. Felt like I'd just escaped arrest. It was odd to feel like a dangerous intruder in a place I called home. Speeding along the empty streets toward downtown Saigon, I just did not feel at ease.

I left town two days later.

Left the atrocious noises, heat, dust, pollution, the insane traffic. The masses spilling out of shops and markets into the streets, from 5:00 or 6:00 in the morning until 10:00 or 11:00 at night. I left them all for Hanoi.

I relished the December coolness, but I was really sad because cement-steel-and-glass blocks were all you could see in many places. Historic houses were being torn down. Beautiful walls and façades full of history, just piles of debris now. They didn't come down during the years of American bombing. But capitalism had arrived, hitting the city badly, and there were foreigners everywhere: Swedish import-exporters; Japanese and Taiwanese real-estate men; Australian oilmen; American lawyers—neo-colonialists, splayed out in the white, newly upholstered backseats of vintage Citroens, driven to government ministries, to factories, to golf courses, or else posturing all over the bars and restaurants, talking money, making deals. And there were French and Dutch backpackers—latter-day hippies supporting lice-infested dorm-like hotels, dining on paté sandwiches and imitation pancakes with coconut syrup, smoking Gauloises, and visiting ancient temples, joking about northern Vietnam's dog-eating habits.

I stayed in the old quarter. The captivating streets and friendly merchants soothed my temper. I forgot about Saigon. I hung out with a bunch of spirited artists and writers. For three weeks they talked and I asked questions, and did some of the talking too. We were trying to figure out where Vietnam was going with all of its isms: Confucianism, Buddhism, Taoism, Catholicism. And communism and capitalism. All imported over two thousand years, coexisting with each other and with Vietnam's own ism, nationalism. The artists and writers gave me gallons of tea. We smoked pack after pack of bad cigarettes, and drank a lot of plum wine. But no one could shed light on any of the isms. We left it to nationalism to fight off the other isms.

I made my way back south. Nationalism wasn't doing well in Hue, the old imperial city. Capitalism had created the sick spectacle in which, for less than fifteen bucks, tourists were served a royal meal while sitting where the Nguyen emperors once sat. Their thrones now belonged to the tourist department. Traditional court musicians squatted on the floor to serenade the feasting tourists. Aging French couples on tour buses couldn't resist this. Sunburned and reddened even more by the warm beer served over ice, they squeezed into royal costumes of gold silk, shoved their heavy asses onto the thrones and became drunken, obnoxious children. You could get away with a lot in Vietnam, provided you had dollars. I left that bizarre scene. Returned to the urban mess called Saigon.

Where capitalism had always been the supreme lord, and where I was to wait for my flight out.

"Meet me at Ciao," Tuan proposed when he called my hotel. I preferred the sidewalk coffee shops with the worn-out miniature stools and metal tables. Ciao was all neon and pastel walls, with too many inept waiters and waitresses serving bad coffee. It was popular with the young, moneyed sets of Saigon, maybe daughters and sons of revolutionaries turned capitalists. The kids were forever watching some Michael Jackson or Tom-and-Jerry videos from TV sets suspended from the ceiling. Or else talking into hand phones. Worse, Ciao was always full of *Viet-Kieu*s in American or Italian clothes and shoes, and hairstyles that looked outrageous in Saigon. Bunch of men looking for love and marriage. Or just to get laid. Always proffering business cards or dollar bills and talking about their latest commercial deals or the Vietnamese beauties they seduced. The deals usually turned out to be exaggerations. The seductions, true.

Tuan was insistent. "I'm meeting some people for dinner nearby. I'll be at Ciao at eight. It's air-conditioned," he said.

I gave in, weaving my way over to the café on a Japanese scooter so old it surprised me that it actually ran. Boys hustling outside my hotel were renting them out for $3 a day. Tuan showed up late, two gorgeous women in tow. We turned into two ugly *Viet-Kieu*s with our beautiful prey. Pale, overweight, we wore T-shirts rather than the dressy ones that were *de rigeur* for Vietnamese men our age. Tuan introduced the women.

Friends of friends. Actresses. I should have guessed. They were stunning. And tall. Neither wore the evening-wear outfits Saigon women can't stay away from. One had a teal, raw-silk ensemble, the other a pair of jeans and a lavender Indian shirt. She wore no makeup, showing off her incredible tan. Her neck, also tanned, was absolutely inviting. She looked cheerful. But behind her gold-rimmed glasses were these woeful eyes that looked as if they might be full of tears.

I lost it. Couldn't talk. Felt just a mess. I was staring at the women, especially My-Kim, the one with the sad eyes. I was looking at those black eyes every time she wasn't looking at me. If she had any sorrow, she carried it in those eyes. They made me think of the blackness of the airport. I kept my head down, pretended to be thinking. Kept staring at her beautiful toes.

Tuan helped by asking about the artists and writers in Hanoi. When he left for the bathroom, My-Kim volunteered to take me to bookstores. "Aren't they closed by now," I asked. "You want to go now?"

"Sure, maybe there's one that's open late."

Her friend laughed. "Nothing's going to be open now. But you two go ahead. We'll wait."

My-Kim and I wandered out, our impromptu walk immediately taking on the colors of a courtship. People stared at us, I stared at my feet, or at My-Kim's, and listened to her talk about her love of reading. I asked her about the books I'd known as a student.

"They didn't teach those books when I went to school," she said, tilting her head.

I wasn't free from my past and forgot how things had

changed. My-Kim had begun school the year I left. Her schoolbooks were all about anti-colonialist and anti-imperialist victories. Revolutionary triumphs. The glorious road to socialism.

We circled the downtown streets and laughed as we passed the bookstores that were closed. The infernal streets of Saigon were now full of excitement. The heat, the dust, the chaos, the crowds. Everything was lovely. Even Ciao. We came back empty-handed. But I didn't care.

It was 10:30 when we decided to leave. Damn scooter wouldn't start. I got tired of kicking the starter pedal so I pushed it. It didn't help. My-Kim came up. One stroke on the pedal and the engine roared. "You're giving it too much gas," she said. I thanked her and, while the street hustlers were laughing, I asked to have breakfast with her. We could go to the bookstores afterward," I said. "I'm married," she said.

"Why didn't you tell me?" I asked Tuan. We were riding around, looking for someplace to have a drink. My-Kim and her friend had left.

"Like you gave me a chance," he said. "Her husband knows my brother."

"Fuck," I said. Didn't know what else to say. We pulled into a side street with plastic tables in the dark. Boys from the beer hall brought four bottles of Tiger. I needed the beer. Same with Tuan. We let long moments go by. Then Tuan started to comment on the meaning of My-Kim's name. Kim is the formal word for American gold: the dollar. And My, the word for America, means beautiful. My-Kim: Beautiful Dollar.

How did I end up coming to Vietnam and getting tangled with a woman named Beautiful Dollar? One who's spoken for?

"I'm sorry," I had said when My-Kim told me she was married. She smiled, but her eyes still had that sadness. "It's not your fault. Breakfast sounds good. Let's talk tomorrow." We agreed on a meeting place, and she rode off into the darkness beyond the downtown streets.

Tuan and I finished the bottles of beer. "My-Kim's husband's a dork. A *Viet-Kieu* from San Jose, an accountant who lucked out. He came home, met My-Kim just three weeks before going back to California."

"You mean she married him after just three weeks?"

"Almost," Tuan said. "He went back to the States, proposed to her on the phone a few months later."

"And she said yes? What is it about the guy?"

"The guy's a fashion plate. Talked a lot about clothes and designers."

"She went for that?"

"I guess. He was here a few months ago, had a ceremony, did the paperwork to sponsor her to go to the States. Now he's not sure."

"What do you mean, not sure?"

"Told me he now has a place to park his body whenever he comes back here. Doesn't sound like he really wants her in the States."

"The sucker."

"Yeah. He was visiting us. Showed us her photos. We sort of laughed. I mean, she's a head taller than the guy. And he's sixteen years older than her. My brother thinks the guy's gonna smother her."

"Fuck," I said. Again.

"Maybe she does love him," Tuan said. "But then why is she seeing you?"

"She saw you tonight," I said.

"I brought her a letter from the guy," Tuan replied.

I started ordering more beer, but Tuan asked for a ride to his mini-hotel. Maybe he sensed that I was wounded. When we rode past the noodle shop, I pulled in knowing we weren't through. We could always talk about the *Viet-Kieu*s who come home to marry Vietnamese women. Many leave the women behind, because they are already married. Or because they just wanted to have fun. Because they really aren't engineers or computer scientists who can support a wife. Such stories are common. But it isn't easy to admit that among your friends was one of those *Viet-Kieus*. We were now implicated. I was, anyhow.

I was early. My-Kim had a flat tire. "I was afraid you wouldn't show up," she said.

"Why?" I asked.

She didn't answer.

"I leave in four days." My-Kim smiled. "I didn't think you would show up either," I said.

We ordered breakfast. My-Kim cut pieces of bread for me and fixed my coffee filter. I poured hot water for her tea. She smiled but didn't thank me. We did things as though we'd always had breakfast together and knew each other's habits. We didn't talk. The sooner we talked, the sooner we'd have to acknowledge the obvious.

The waiter cleared the table. My-Kim crossed her arms and held herself in. I smoked the cigarettes that were left in my pack and ordered another coffee. I asked her about being an actress.

"It's really hopeless here," she said.

"What do you plan to do in the States?"

"I don't know. I'm taking English lessons."

My-Kim didn't really have any skills that would be helpful in America. She had been an athlete in college, and afterward had become a physical therapist for handicapped children. Acting was a new thing.

"D'you want to go to college?"

"Yes. But I'll have a kid as soon as I get there."

I felt weak in the stomach. "Is that what he wants?" I asked. It was the first time I'd acknowledged her husband.

"I don't know. I think so." She placed her hand on mine. "Minh, I'll show you my acting pictures." She pulled an envelope out of her handbag.

"My-Kim, do you really want a kid?"

She set the pictures on the table. "If it'll make him happy."

"What about you?" I was troubled by the Buddhist attitude, or was it Vietnamese fatalism.

"What about me? Look, this is from a recent film. And that one, that's from a couple of years ago. *Con nit ghe, anh ha?* Don't I look childish?"

I went through the pictures, admiring her beauty. I kept looking from the pictures to her eyes, trying to see what she was suggesting about her future that I might accept. My-Kim fell silent. When I reached the end of her fashion photos, I found some wedding pictures. "Did you want me to see these?" I asked.

"If you want to."

My-Kim looked slim and dazzling in an embroidered tunic of triumphant red. But her eyes were strange, uncomprehending. The makeup didn't cover the innocence in her face. Or the sadness. I tried to stay calm, said a few words about the majestic dress. The only words I could manage.

"He's standing on a stool," she said. I turned my attention to her husband. The San Jose accountant looked awkward. "He wouldn't let me wear a tiara," she said. "I'm towering over him as it is."

"Do you love him?" I surprised myself with the directness of my question. I was trying to project the notion that I could take an answer, any answer, from her. Her hesitation was hard to sit through. Then I felt bad for the satisfaction her answer gave me. "I'm neither in love with him nor do I love him," My-Kim said.

The satisfaction evaporated. I thought about My-Kim's fate, and those of countless women who marry just to leave Vietnam. "Do you really want to come to the States?"

My-Kim's eyes looked full of tears again. "I don't know," she said. "I needed some stability, I guess. He asked. I said yes." She had crossed her arms in front of her chest again, and avoided looking at me.

"I don't think you should have a child, My-Kim, unless . . ."

She looked up. "It's the only way I'll stay with him."

"My-Kim. I mean, what do you want me to say? What do you expect. . . ."

My-Kim gathered her photos. "I know what you want to say," she said, her voice soft, resigned. "You don't have to say it. Should I take you to the bookstores?"

I paid the bill and we left. We spent the rest of the morning looking at books and talking about the revival of Vietnamese literature under Vietnam's new policies. We went back to pretending there was nothing awkward about being together. But My-Kim was doing a better job, at times casually hanging her hand on the crook of my arm, or placing it on my back, drawing me to one book or another. I no longer had the ability to quietly accept everything that life hands us. I was boiling with questions. My-Kim kept saying, *thoi, hoi lam chi*? Please, why ask? She always managed to stop me short, calmly and comfortingly.

At lunch, I started again. "Maybe I shouldn't have asked you to meet me for breakfast."

Very quietly, My-Kim said my name. "Minh. I am grateful for these moments. I meet a lot of *Viet-Kieu*s. I've always been allergic to them. I know the horror stories. But I've made a choice. I have no idea what it's like in San Jose. Good, bad, I don't know. I don't want to start having any regrets. Not this early."

"I'm sorry."

"I just hate myself."

"For what?"

"For not waiting," My-Kim said. "What do you want?"

I hadn't expected the question.

"I don't want to be pitied. Be honest."

I really was at a loss. I told My-Kim so. Then I said, "I have four days left here."

"Three. But that's better than none."

"Beyond that, I don't even know. I wish I knew what's really going on. You just seem sad. I wish I could take some of it away."

"Thanks." That was all she said. And somehow, it cut through me, and it was enough to want to change my ticket back to California.

"I have to go to a wedding tonight," My-Kim said. "Wish I didn't have to. I don't want to lie, so I won't bring you. But tomorrow, I've no plans for breakfast."

"Do you want to?"

"Of course I do. If you want to. Tomorrow night, I'm supposed to be at the New World Hotel for a gig at 6:00. Will you take me?"

"Yes, of course. You said honest. About what?"

"Your emotions. It's nice that you've come back to Vietnam. It's really hopeless here. But no one wants pity."

"You're fucked," Tuan said.

I'd had too much to drink to say anything. We were in one of Saigon's countless beer halls. My-Kim and I had had another silent breakfast that morning. We rode around to a string of cafés and ice-cream shops, had lunch, and an early dinner. Then I took her to the New World Hotel. The ten-story building cast an ugly shadow over the Saigon horizon. My-Kim didn't want me to bring her inside. We stood by the fountain at the entrance. A group of Vietnamese in their Sunday best were having photographs taken near the fountain. The hotel guests, mostly Westerners, gave us mocking looks.

I rode off on her motorcycle to meet Tuan. He wasn't in a mood to comfort me. "You're fucked. I just hope she'll be fine after you leave."

"I just wish I could help her."

"You're pitying her, Minh. Why don't you . . ."

"I tried changing my ticket," I said.

"Another week won't change things. Might as well go back to California."

"And then what?"

"See how you feel. You've only known her for two days."

"I think it's sad. To have a baby just to stay married. Or to please the dork."

"Nothing you can do," Tuan said. He quoted from *The Tale of Kieu*, Vietnam's classic verse epic. *Ma dan loi, quy dua duong. Lai tim nhung loi doan truong ma di.* Ghosts and devils lead the way. For she is again upon the path of sorrow. "Don't her eyes tell you she's the kind that would go from one misery to another? I wonder what happened to her before she met the dork. I doubt she's had a lot of fun. Now it's you."

"Nothing you can do about fate, man."

"That's really lame. So now you're back to being Vietnamese and blaming fate for everything. What about the *Viet-Kieu* that wanted to help?"

"Tuan," I said. "Lay off. I just don't know what to do."

There was really nothing I could do. I asked Tuan to come with me to the shops the next day. I wanted to buy a tiara. I thought that would be a gift that could tell My-Kim I wanted her to stand as tall as she possibly could.

"You're cruel," Tuan said. "You're just thinking of yourself, Minh. You want to show yourself a savior. You know you're safe. You don't have to marry her. You're worse than those *Viet-Kieu*s. You're worse than the dork."

I felt worse than the dork when I went to pick up My-Kim. I hated him, hated the Korean airline. I was sick of not knowing what to do. I did not know about the streets of Saigon. They had seemed so sweet when I was riding around with My-Kim on the backseat. Now they were crammed with people oblivious to what I was going through. I resented them. I was upset with the odd and cruel way life was in my homeland. Or the odd way of life in my homeland and the cruelty in me.

My-Kim was waiting outside the New World. She smiled. Everything seemed better. "How was your evening?" I asked her. "Are you tired?"

"It was all right. Take me somewhere for a drink."

I brought her to Gigi's, a bar owned by a *Viet-Kieu* I'd known in California. I had a letter for her. We rode past the pedicab drivers and the hustlers who get paid to park the scooters outside Gigi's. My-Kim was resting her chin on my shoulder. It could be embarrassing, I warned myself. Gigi's was the gathering place for expats and *Viet-Kieu*s who often show up late at night with their girlfriends, some of whom barely disguised the fact that they were prostitutes. I convinced myself that My-Kim and I were friends. Nothing to fear. Damn what other people thought, anyway.

"*Roi, dot duoc mot em thom qua,*" a hustler said. I felt sheepish, but My-Kim laughed, unfazed. When she got off the motorcycle, she turned to me. "*Em thom khong anh?*" she asked.

That's it. The guy's picked up a nice-smelling babe, the hustler had said. Nice-smelling. Vietnamese slang for a beautiful woman. I was hoping My-Kim hadn't heard the comment. But she had turned and asked, "Am I nice-smelling?"

I wanted to offer her a compliment, to say she was beautiful. But nice-smelling wasn't the way I could do it. I smiled and guided My-Kim through the double doors of Gigi's.

Gigi stood up from her table, kissed me on both cheeks and hugged me. I leaned over to introduce My-Kim; the place was real noisy.

"Did you just come from California too?" Gigi asked in English.

My-Kim smiled.

"No, no," I said. "She's a friend."

Gigi winked at me. It didn't escape My-Kim's eyes. We sat down. Gigi shouted questions at me in English. I pretended not to hear, repeating her questions, answering in Vietnamese. My-Kim leaned over and whispered, "You don't have to translate."

A waitress brought the drink menu. "What would you like?" I asked.

"I'd like very much to have whatever you're going to have." The sweetness in her voice carried a promise, an acknowledgment of conspiracy, of intimacy. I was amazed. She'd managed all of that in a sentence meant to hide the fact that she could not make heads or tails out of the cocktail list.

I decided not to have a whiskey sour, since that would involve explaining it to My-Kim. "A beer," I said. "I'm having a beer. Would you like one?"

Gigi left us. My-Kim told me about her evening. She and some twenty other actresses had been asked to serve brandy and wine at a cocktail party for some foreign investors. In the darkness of Gigi's bar, her eyes had turned a deeper black. They carried all the sorrow I had detected before. And all the sorrow of a postwar nation, independent, but needing to please foreigners with money. The most beautiful women in Saigon had been used to court foreigners and their dollars. I started to count myself among that crowd of foreigners. Next to me sat one of those beautiful women, nursing her grief. I drank my beer, smoked my cigarette. I felt ugly. Her name meant Beautiful Dollar.

My-Kim shocked me, suggesting that we visit her parents. I was dropping her off outside her rented room in a house stuck between a dozen two-story buildings in a twisting and muddy alley far from downtown Saigon.

"What if they find out?" I said.

"Find out what? I would like you to meet them, very much. Please," she said.

We had a quick breakfast early the next day and headed out. Her parents lived in a village by the side of a dusty highway, forty minutes from Saigon. My-Kim's sister, who owned a noodle shop that served the carpenters from the lumberyard next door, laid out a massive meal. At 10:00 in the morning, I wasn't all that hungry. My-Kim left me with the villagers and their questions about life in America, the Beautiful Country. She joked with her father, a frail man with an extraordinary smile, and seemed in no hurry. Later I found out he'd been imprisoned by four regimes in Vietnam. Under Ho Chi Minh, because he was suspected of working for the French. Under the Ngo Dinh Diem regime, he was a police officer imprisoned for opposing the suppression of the

Buddhists, even though a devout Catholic himself. The Nguyen Van Thieu government kept him for several years under charges of involvement in a coup. The communists sent him to a re-education camp for eight years for being a policeman in the two previous regimes. Three additional years for illegally raising and selling pigs. "I'm 70 years old," he said. "Been in prison for as many years as I've been out."

I mumbled my congratulations on his health and offered my sunglasses for his bad eyes. My-Kim's mother waited until I was leaving to ask a favor: "Please tell Long we said hello. We're anxious that he bring My-Kim to America. We've heard all the stories." She lowered her voice. "He's not already married, or anything like that, is he?"

"No," I said. "Nothing like that."

We rode back to Saigon under the midday sun. I couldn't blame My-Kim for telling her parents I was a friend of her husband. But I was worried.

"He never talks to my parents," she said.

For the rest of the journey, I kept asking about her father's years in prison. I realized that, for My-Kim, communism, Catholicism, or Buddhism didn't matter. Her love for her father included his image as a suffering hero. All that time I was trying to make sense of all the isms in Vietnam. I'd forgotten about Vietnamese romanticism.

All you want to do in Saigon at 2:00 in the afternoon is to sit inside a refrigerator. My-Kim promised ice cream, provided I came with her to do an errand.

"Under the sun, now?"

"Please," she said. "It won't take long."

It took an hour and a half. And all my efforts. But I wasn't unhappy. In twelve hours, I was going to get on a flight and go away. My-Kim had to drop off a certificate that she had picked up at her parents'. It was from the authorities in the village of her birth, by the side of the dusty highway. It stated that they had no record she was married. We went to the agency that was processing her papers for departure to the U.S.

There was a massive waiting room with sorry-looking benches. It looked like the inside of a church, but the benches were inches apart. At least three hundred people were pressed against one another, falling asleep on those benches, clutching plastic bags and folders containing all the papers that showed their connections to someone or something in America. Former employees of American firms and governmental agencies in South Vietnam. Former soldiers and officers of the South Vietnamese army, America's ally. Former political prisoners. Relatives of *Viet-Kieu*s. And women in My-Kim's situation. The three ceiling fans made a joke of the sweating people.

My-Kim and I sat in the back. She held my hand and used her papers to fan me. She glanced at me occasionally, wordless. It didn't escape either of us that we were in the most remarkable and uncanny circumstance. We were spending our last moments together in this oven of a room, waiting for confirmation that she had submitted a piece of paper in order to join someone else on the other side of the world. My side of the world. A life sentence, she had said at one point. It was funny when she said it. When her name was called, we looked at each other and laughed. She walked off.

My-Kim reneged on her promise. No ice cream. She took me to a karaoke café. Saigon is karaoke town. I'd never been to one and was taken aback by the darkness inside. By the time my eyes adjusted, I no longer minded the gaudy drapes, dirty walls, and vinyl seats. My-Kim selected songs from before the war. Others sang more recent ones. Over two million have left the country. There were songs that spoke to the hearts of those far from home. Songs about Saigon's wind-blown streets and the midday rooster calls, or the horse-drawn merchant carts. Songs about those left behind and those about to leave. Terribly sentimental songs. But they made sense. Nationalism will always have a role in Vietnam, but sentimentalism was primordial.

I understood that the people whose lives in Vietnam were full of misery could once in a while proclaim their sorrow out loud. Most didn't sing very well, but they sang with all their sincerity, all their emotions. I believed so, for when My-Kim began to sing again, I wanted to believe she was able to let go of her sorrow.

I forgot the time. When she placed her fingers on my knees and let her voice tell me I now had "a world to leave, and a world to come back to," I believed there was a heart in my homeland.

I bribed the customs and immigration officer at the Saigon airport. Ten dollars. He stamped my passport, waved me through. No one bothered with my bags. It was past 1:00 in the morning. There was no bar or restaurant. The one souvenir shop was closed. My-Kim didn't have a phone.

I wrote a letter and asked an airport janitor to mail it.

Offered her five dollars. "For my wife," I said. The woman looked the envelope over. "Oh. It's local. But you've given me too much money. And your wife, she has a nice name. My-Kim." I thanked the woman, and left to board the plane. I had a window seat, but there was nothing but darkness outside.

It made me think again of My-Kim's eyes. Eyes the color of sorrow.

I turned away, reached for the book in my bag. The plane was taxiing. I fastened my seat belt and opened the book to where I'd placed two envelopes. The one with the San Jose address I put away. It contained proof of papers submitted to immigration authorities in Vietnam. The other one, with my name on it, I held on my lap. The stewardess was making some kind of announcement in Korean. I peered again into the darkness when the plane took off.

The stewardess was now saying, "Welcome to Asiana flight 606, Ho Chi Minh City to Los Angeles. The estimated duration of our flight today will be sixteen hours, forty minutes. Please refrain from smoking for the entire duration of the flight."

I held onto the envelope, and wished I'd had another smoke before boarding.

Dark Wood and Shadows

Andrew Q. Lam

AFTER A STORMY flight back from Saigon, where we had been visiting sick relatives, our Cessna landed with a thud on the muddy landing strip of the Cam Ly airport. Outside, a curtain of rain moved softly across the smoky gray sky, welcoming us back to this high plateau of persistent fog and whispering pine forests. The plane ran swiftly toward the control tower while brown water spurted under its white metallic wings. When it slowed it let out a fierce roar—the sound of a wounded beast—then came to a shuddering stop.

Now that we were safely on the ground, Maman exhaled and leaned back in her seat. With a swift, expert gesture from her hand she snapped open her alligator purse, took out a money envelope, and gave it to the pilot. Beyond the plane's windshield swayed the dark figures of Uncle Lau and Uncle Hien, our servants, who stood by our Plymouth and a couple of rusty army trucks. They rushed toward the plane, black umbrellas in hand, as the propeller completed its final spin.

The Cessna's door sprang open. A cold blast of moist air rushed in, bringing the fragrance of musty earth and pine trees. I could hear the raging Cam Ly falls echoing from behind the green hills. Uncle Lau was the first to greet us. With a pale and trembling hand he held an umbrella over the open door. Then, through his dark, shivering lips, he uttered something quite unintelligible.

"What is it?" Maman asked, stepping down from the plane, alarmed at his behavior. "Is everything all right?"

"Madame, dear Madame," he mumbled as a wisp of cloud escaped his mouth, "she wore a red *jupe*. I swear, Madame, I saw her with my own eyes."

Uncle Hien shook his head slightly, stepping past Uncle Lau just in time to help Brother Tuan, who jumped carelessly out after Maman, landing with one foot in a mud puddle. The pilot, in the meantime, had finished packing our valises into the car's trunk and trotted off toward the army PX.

"Who wore a red *jupe*?" Maman sounded annoyed, having endured a turbulent flight, and now this. Uncle Lau had always been a little *toqué*, talking to himself frequently. Yet this unusually abnormal behavior made everyone curious.

"Is my Papa all right?" Sister Ngoc asked. She sat on the ledge of the plane's door frame, hesitating to jump and risk ruining her favorite pink *ao dai** dress that Maman had sewn.

"Hush." Maman touched her. Then, with her piercing glance she turned again to Uncle Lau. "Now, who wore a red dress? My husband's new girlfriend? Who?"

Uncle Lau cringed under her stare. The umbrella he held wobbled in his hand. "No, Madame, no such girlfriends. Your . . ." He hesitated, his eyes filled with fear.

"Talk!" Maman ordered. She was angry now, her voice

**ao dai:* traditional silk dress of fluttery panels, worn with pantaloons.

becoming a pitch higher. She smoothed back a few loose strands of hair from her forehead, faced him fully, and waited for his answer. The flaps of her embroidered *ao dai* fluttered like the panicked wings of butterflies. . . .

"Your daughter, dear Madame," he blurted, a grown man ready to cry. Sister Ngoc and I stared at each other, not exactly sure what he meant—he had seen Sister Ngoc almost every day since we moved to Dalat. In unison we began to giggle at his strange response while from inside the gray Plymouth my oblivious brother with his smiling face yelled for us to hurry. Uncle Hien, who was the braver servant, had just returned with his umbrella for my sister and me. We pretended to be stranded peasants in the Mekong flood, waiting for rescue.

"Please pay him no mind, Madame," Uncle Hien advised, his dark umbrella covering the sky. "He talks shadows and he talks winds."

But Maman ignored Uncle Hien and continued to press at a fearful Uncle Lau. "My daughter, you mean Ngoc?" She sounded much calmer for some reason, pointing at my sister, whose sandaled feet dangled above the muddy water.

"No, not right, Madame," Uncle Lau shook his head vigorously. His whole thin frame seemed to shake with him. "The dead one . . ."

We stopped giggling. Sister Ngoc halted her legs in mid-swing, then raised them back over the plane's ledge and into the protection of her embracing, wool-sweatered arms. I heard a muted shriek from my own mouth and felt something cold rise in me as I leaned closer to her. Uncle Lau was no longer funny. There was an eerie silence among all of us and I suddenly heard again the waterfall's soft rumble against the distant hills and obscured thatched hamlets. Maman took a small step forward, swaying a little. Her face paled suddenly; it mirrored the sky.

"Talk of lies!" Maman exclaimed. "You're lying." But Uncle Lau just shook and shook his skinny head.

"My dead daughter," she mumbled to herself a moment later, her eyes gazing at the verdant slopes. Then suddenly she seemed panicked. "Dear God! I burned a red dress for her last year."

She turned to Uncle Hien and grabbed his arm. "What day is it today, Uncle Hien?"

"The 18th of August, Madame," Uncle Hien told her while helping Sister Ngoc and me down from the plane.

"Sufferings, oh sufferings!" Maman cried softly. A million tiny raindrops covered her curly black hair. "I completely neglected Nga's death anniversary. I was so busy with my ailing cousins . . . Uncle Lau, when did you . . . see her?"

"Four days ago, Madame," Uncle Lau told her.

"That would be the 14th, a day after her death anniversary," Maman whispered, no longer sounding surprised. She sobbed very quietly with the rain.

In the car we were quiet. A still shaken Uncle Lau sat in front with Uncle Hien, their m-16s between them. In the back, Maman sat with my brother and me on her right and Sister Ngoc on her left. The rain fell heavier, its drops gathering momentum and tapping sonorously on the car's roof. We rode down a gentle slope, leaving the blurry military airport with its simple wooden barracks and muddy landing strips to drown in the rain.

"Uncle Lau," Maman ordered, "tell me from beginning to end what happened. And mind you not to forget a single thing."

"Yes, Madame." His voice squeaked as he struggled to turn around and face us. His scrawny profile and long skinny neck reminded me of the funny rooster Sister Ngoc and I had raised. One of Papa's chauffeurs had run over it last summer—Maman had thought it was a deliberate act because the bird had crowed so loudly and so early in the morning and had wakened everyone in the servant quarters and soldier barracks. Presently, Uncle Lau cleared his throat, his Adam's apple vibrating visibly on his neck. He did this often. While doing our laundry, he sang modern theater, *cai luong*, his favorite pastime. He could be completely eloquent when he performed. I giggled but Maman put her hand on mine and I immediately became quiet.

In a warm and solemn voice he began, "It was like this. You remember, Madame, that the week before last, when you and the children were preparing to go to Saigon, you told me and Hien here to guard the house in case of any danger to the General. Well, we did just that, alternating sleeping in that icy study there down the hall. We had set up an army cot by the rosewood altar of Miss Nga, near the old fireplace.

"The children used the blackboard in the study so often that chalk powder is everywhere—on the floor, over the table, in the fireplace, among the books, on the shelves— everything's gotten covered with a white layer of dust. Of course, I cleaned everything the first day I slept there, wiping the place spotless as you would have liked it. Then, strangely enough, when it was Hien's turn, he complained that there was chalk powder on the floor and even on the cot.

"Well, I know nobody dared use the board, and certainly not my filial children, they wouldn't step foot in your respectable house without your word, Madame. Still, it doesn't explain where the chalk powder came from at all.

"Chalk is chalk, but duty *is* duty so I came right back the next morning and cleaned the place up. With my rag and chicken feather broom I started this laborious work. That night, that wintry night, however, something strange, very strange, happened. Dear Madame, I still am scared to death thinking about it. You see, it was like this. . . ." At this point, he made a smacking sound with the inside of his cheeks. The rain tapped on the car's roof to accompany his voice.

"That night Dalat was full of thick fog. And the wind, it howled and whimpered right there among the tops of the pine trees. I left my family back in the quarters and went up to the house with my m-16. Before I left, my poor wife had some strange premonitions, she kept saying: 'You shouldn't go, you shouldn't go.'" He copied Auntie Lau's voice, which was a piercing and commanding voice. He had perfected it and we all laughed, including Maman. "She cried, 'The General is nowhere home for you to protect. Protect yourself and stay here with your devoted wife, don't leave. There isn't even a shadow up at that big empty and old house. What for you leave? Stay home with me!'

"But I would listen to no woman's word, Madame. It

was my turn to guard the house, so out I went, through the thick fog and slapping wind, up the steps into the kitchen, down the empty living room, up that squeaky staircase and through that creaky door and right into the study. Sure enough, there was plenty of chalk on the cot but I just dusted it off with my hands, turned off the light and lay down with my gun and pulled the army blanket over me and went to sleep. The wind was strong and beastly outside, but I didn't mind it. I am a soldier after all.

"Well, everything seemed to be fine and I slept deliciously. Then, something—I still don't know what—woke me up. It sounded as if someone had whispered in my ear, so I prayed to the saints and buddhas that it was only the wind. I didn't know what time it was but I knew it was still early in the morning because outside the window it was near pitch-black. All I could see really was the dim yellow lightbulb glowing behind the trees near the soldiers' barracks. For a while nothing happened and I was about to fall back asleep when I . . . I felt something terribly cold pulling at my right ankle. It felt like a small icy hand. And I couldn't move. All I could do was crane my neck over the blanket and open my eyes as wide as I could to see what it was.

"Oh God, Madame, I saw her then. She was glowing in this strange soft light, this little girl, about six or seven, and I could barely make out this red *jupe* that she was wearing. I was so scared my mouth was just open wide, and, if you forgive me for saying, Madame, my spit was running out on both sides of my gaping mouth. She was just standing there, this little girl, right at the other end of my cot holding on to my foot, crying. . . . Her hair was long and silky and her face was ivory white.

"Right away I knew it was her. I just knew it was your deceased daughter. She materialized before me as a beautiful and delicate child, a china doll. But I was paralyzed. My jaw was locked open, my blood froze in my veins, and I think my hair stood straight up from my scalp. Like a log I just lay there, and I stared at her while she cried. An eternity passed before she stopped crying and finally she looked up at me." Here Uncle Lau began to speak in a very soft voice. It was almost a whisper but audible enough in the car for all of us to hear. Maman was squeezing my hand very tight.

"*Uncle Lau. It's sooo cold. I am forgotten, Uncle Lau. Maman has forgotten me. Please, light an incense to warm my lonely home once more. Please, I am sooo cold.*'

"With that, Madame, she let go of my ankle. Then, she turned and floated toward the fireplace where her dark altar stood. Like a wind-blown puff of winter cloud she faded away. Oh, Madame, I tried to gather my calm then, hoping that she wouldn't come back a second time and scare me to death. When I finally could move I stood up and turned on the study's light switch. With all the courage in me, I approached the altar and took three incense sticks from the bag and lit them. I prayed to her, I said: 'Oh Miss Nga, I now burn the incense for you. Please, I beg of you, do not scare me again for I am a weak man. I am a devout Buddhist and have a wife and three children to care for. Please don't take my soul away. I will bring you some offerings come morning. Please, Miss Nga,' I said and then bowed three times and placed the incense in the cassolette in front of that altar. Then, well, Madame, seeing that my wife had made some sense after all, and with the General . . . well, with nobody in the house, I took the liberty of staying home myself and protecting my poor wife and children.

"The next morning I came right back with my wife and we brought some fruits to offer your daughter while you were away. I knew you wouldn't object. Then the past few nights, Hien here has volunteered to take my shifts as well since he said that Miss Nga wouldn't bother him now that she had received some offerings. But I made sure, you can trust me, Madame, I made sure that Hien lit incense every night for her. . . ."

Uncle Lau's tale ended. To acknowledge it Maman nodded and he, seeing no further instruction, turned again to face the car's windshield. A faint smell of *ruou de,* the servants' favorite moonshine, had become increasingly strong as Uncle Lau spoke, and it lingered in the air. Repulsed, I turned then to look at Brother Tuan, who sat to my right. He was breathing on the car's window, turning it into a fog-filled writing board. He drew pictures of airplanes and tanks and guns on the obscured window's glass. With each stroke, he revealed a rushing green, gray, and wet world outside, the animated images glowing with the color of sweet nature.

Though Nga had been my sister, I had never seen her. She died as an infant of some brain disease a year before I was born. For her light skin Maman had named her Nga, which means ivory. She had dark silky hair when she was born—Maman insisted that she would have been very tall and pretty had she lived. Nga was a good child, Maman always told me. She never cried or demanded so much attention like me. I had responded always by whining and stomping my feet until Maman laughed and held me in her arms, reassuring me that I was still her favorite son.

Every year, on Sister Nga's death anniversary, Maman bought paper dresses, toys, and money to burn for her in the spirit world so that she could have all the comforts like the rest of us. We hadn't always been prosperous, Maman told us; we were poor then—Papa was only a lieutenant colonel—and we had no money, no chauffeur, no cars. When it was time to give birth to Sister Nga, Maman had to take the pedicab alone to the hospital. Then when Sister Nga died, Maman bought a piece of ivory and carved on it Nga's name for worshipping. She could have been saved, Maman often argued, had we enough money and connections to take her to Europe. But Papa had said that there was nothing anybody could do and that no doctors would have known what to do with such a rare brain disease.

Papa was promoted to brigadier general a year after I was born. Our lives started to change for the better as he received more privileges, being the commander of the 9th Division in Sadec. A few years later, as a lieutenant general, he administered the Vo Bi National Military Academy in Dalat. We received a French villa, some horses, and a private helicopter. But Maman never forgot about my sister. When we were moving to Dalat, the first item Maman packed was the altar, despite Papa's objection. Papa thought it was silly to hold on to the dead. He said it was best to place the altar in a quiet temple since we moved around so much. "Let her spirit rest," he would shout, but Maman was relentless. They argued and argued, but somehow Maman always ended up winning.

Now, in light of everything, it was scary to think that my dead sister's ghost might roam our villa, demanding attention from Maman like the rest of us kids. I closed

my eyes and tried to think of her living above the fireplace inside that dark wooden altar that resembled a
miniature Buddhist temple. It was a small altar with a
curving roof and two little columns carved into shapes of
dragons and phoenixes. Between the columns stood a
bronze cassolette filled with burnt joss sticks and gray-
brown ashes. But the altar's sacred dark interior held
nothing but that ivory tablet, standing like a miniature
tombstone. Could that piece of ivory embody her spirit?

"And you, Uncle Hien," Maman's voice broke the
silence, "did you see anything strange?"

"No, Madame," Uncle Hien answered with his eyes on
the road. His face in the rearview mirror was dark and ex-
pressionless.

"You mean my daughter did not grab your ankle or
scare you as well?" Maman pressed on.

"No, Madame. Perhaps because my spirit is strong
ghosts do not bother me."

"Is that so?" Maman mused.

"But Madame," Uncle Lau now turned around again
and interrupted, "I saw her." He pointed at his face. "I
saw her with my own eyes."

"Yes, I know," Maman nodded. "But I am no longer
asking you."

"Uncle Hien," Maman continued, "you've nothing to
report?"

"No, Madame. Not about ghosts." He steered expertly
past a slow-moving army truck as he reached inside his
khaki shirt and pulled out an envelope. "The General,
however, has asked me to tell you that he won't be back
from conference in Nha Trang for a few more days. He
told me to give this letter to you. . . ."

"Oh?" Maman asked quickly as she took the envelope without opening it. She would never read anything from Papa in front of us. "Did my husband know anything about this . . . apparition?"

"No, Madame."

"Just as well." Maman was pensive. "But why did you volunteer to take Uncle Lau's place instead of staying in your barrack?"

"Because, Madame," Uncle Hien's voice rang in a warm baritone, "the barracks are crowded and drafty and noisy; and because of the ongoing bingo games. I can never sleep when Lau here comes over and yells out his bingo numbers in verses."

"Is that so?" was Maman's only comment, but I laughed and laughed. Brother Tuan slapped his knee and Sister Ngoc kept saying, "Shame, shame," while Uncle Lau seemed to shrink in the front seat. It was true, Uncle Lau tended to be very poetic and loud with bingo games, as with everything else—but especially with bingo numbers. He could sing about them as if they were characters in his well-memorized *cai luong* plays.

After a while a cold and embracing silence enshrouded us again like an opaque mosquito net. Under Maman's hand, mine felt cold and bloodless. The rain had lessened, and the car rumbled and hummed as we neared home, its tires splashing in water-filled potholes and my heart absorbing each pulsing shock. We drove past the Xuan-Huong Lake where the drifting fog caressed its surface. It was late in the afternoon, the sky was dark and miserable, and the water reflected it.

Past the waving wipers I saw a stirring landscape filled with half-hidden villas behind tall pine trees and wooden fences. We were moving uphill where a few small shrines decorated with colorful leis and wreaths of yellow flowers stood beside the ascending road. The local people had built these small whitewashed shrines to pay homage to the numerous people who had died in car and motorcycle accidents on these slippery roads. If the dead ones were remembered, Uncle Lau had once explained to me, they would not come back and cause more accidents.

We were almost there. The red roof of our villa loomed into view above the pine trees; next came the wooden shutters covering the windows and balconies on the second floor; then our green garden with Mickey Mouse swings bloomed to our right. The car made a sharp turn toward the barbed-wire gate, and a young smiling soldier jumped out from his little wooden post, his rifle and guitar slung loosely behind him. He pulled hard at the gate until it slid to the side, then he saluted us as we drove past. Sister Ngoc waved and Maman nodded. On the empty stone yard, white twirling mist rose to welcome us home. The Plymouth drew up to the lichened stone steps and came to a stop.

Maman leaned forward and tapped Uncle Lau on the shoulder with a few large bills. "Uncle Lau," she said. "Could you go, please, to the market and get me some paper offerings, some fruit, and candles as well. I want to offer a modest death anniversary for my daughter . . . even if it's late. And thank you for your offerings."

"Yes, Madame," said Uncle Lau enthusiastically.

Someone had left the windows open in the cold and damp study and the mist from the rain came settling in. There was a musty smell of damp wood here, and when

Maman shut the windows, it seemed that a part of the wet sky was captured inside. I looked up then to the altar on the fireplace. It stood as it always did, ominous, hollow, and dark. Its dragons with sparkling mother-of-pearl scales had their jaws wide open, ready to snap at nonbelievers. I had always felt numb and cold when I looked at it. Maman lit a few incense sticks, and the smoke twirled and whirled upward to the already darkened ceiling. Their pungent fragrance, mixed with the scent of cedar, suspended in the cold moist air.

While I stood behind Maman and listened to her prayers, Brother Tuan and Sister Ngoc gathered by the blackboard with mischievous smiles. They scooped the chalk dust from the board's ledge and smeared it on their giggling faces. When they motioned me to join them, I shook my head. I had a need to be near Maman, to be safe. They were waiting to ambush Uncle Lau, his footsteps echoing nearer from the hallway.

As Uncle Lau stepped in with his wicker basket full of flowers, mangoes, paper toys, and mock dresses, they both screamed and jumped with ghastly faces and clawed hands before him. As if shocked by high voltage, he jerked backward, screaming, his eyes bulging. A mango fell from the basket and hit the floor with a thud.

"Stop that!" Maman turned angrily. There was something foreboding in her glare. Incense smoke drifted lazily behind her. "Go wash your faces, put on some new clothes, and come back to pay tribute to your sister. All of you!"

"Yes, Maman," Brother Tuan and Sister Ngoc mumbled in unison, their heads bowed apologetically. When they left, I followed them, leaving Maman and the dark altar, and we passed Uncle Lau, who bent down and picked the mango from the floor as he mumbled about having a weak heart.

Later, when we returned, two flickering candles burned dreamily on their lotus-flower-shaped stands at each side of the altar. Shadows and lights played among the altar's curving dark wood. It was near dusk outside and the windows glowed in soft pink tones. Uncle Lau was helping Maman, who had on a white silk *ao dai* dress, as they prepared for the late death anniversary. A few mangoes and lotus flowers lay in a large china dish on a table covered with white cloth. We had showered and combed our hair and dressed in our best clothes: Sister Ngoc in her light blue skirt, Brother Tuan and I in our black *complets* with black clip-on ties. We stood in a line behind Maman, from oldest to youngest, and faced the altar. When it was finally my turn, Maman handed me a burning incense stick and told me what to say. "Sister Nga, please forgive us," I chanted, eyes half closed, my hands clasping the incense like a magic wand. "And please protect us and bless us with good fortune." Then I added, "And please, if you are a ghost, don't come back and grab Maman's ankles." I bowed three times to my sister of the altar. I imagined her acknowledging my prayer from that blurry ivory tablet deep inside the mysterious darkness.

Maman stood quietly in front of the fireplace, her eyes transfixed on the shifting and coiling smoke. When we burned the paper offerings for Sister Nga in the fireplace —the best part of doing offerings—Maman cried. The colorful paper *ao dai* dresses and dolls with conical hats and mock paper money caught fire and emitted a brilliant color of gold, with a slight tint of green. Maman's gentle face glowed warmly, and tears shimmered in her eyes. Somewhere down the hall, a wooden shutter, loose from its hinge, flapped rhythmically against the outside wall with the flirting wind.

After a while, there was a knock on the door and we all turned to see Uncle Hien standing like a statue with a small hammer in his hand. "Come in, Uncle," Maman ordered. "You can begin in a moment. We're almost finished."

As he approached I stared hard at his wooden face, curious to see what his task would be. He didn't acknowledge anyone; he just stood to the side with Uncle Lau. When the last incense expired, Maman turned to Uncle Hien and gestured with her hand, "You can begin now."

Uncle Hien nodded and, after he had moved aside the candles, the cassolette, and the offering table, traced his callused hands along the sides of the altar. Then, with his hammer, he began to pull out the nails that held the altar to the wall.

"Maman, what's he doing?" Brother Tuan ventured the question that I wanted to ask.

"He's taking the altar away," Maman answered matter-of-factly, "to the Su-Nu temple in the mountains."

"Why, Maman?" I blurted.

"We are moving soon to Da Nang. Your father received orders from the headquarters in Saigon. He's to command the First Division. . . . It seems that there's a lot of fighting lately. Sufferings . . ." Maman sounded very tired as she held out Papa's letter. "And this time, I am not bringing Nga's altar with us. I think your father is right after all. We mustn't burden ourselves with ghosts."

Uncle Hien started to hammer on the sides of the altar to loosen it. The sharp pounding echoed in the room and the ivory table collapsed inside the dark wooden house. Uncle Lau, after a moment of hesitation, was now assisting his companion. With his help, the last nail that held the altar to the wall gave way with a small screech. In a brief moment, the two soldiers had carried the bulky wooden box downstairs. In its place remained only a white space.

The room seemed much brighter and warmer now without Sister Nga's altar and I could almost taste the fresh, cool air. I was no longer afraid. Instead, as I stared into that white space on the wall, I suddenly thought of Papa. I imagined him flying his helicopter inside a bank of fog. And below that fog where the fireplace had been a minute ago now glowed the embers of a burning city.

And Maman, as she turned to leave the study, crumpled the letter and dropped it onto that dying city. My heart started to beat wildly as I bent closer to observe the paper. A few of Papa's words stood out on the wrinkled letter that squirmed in the heat and turned darker and darker in the streaming black smoke. It said something ... *shadows* ... something ... *war*. ... But before I could make sense of the words, a fierce, brilliant flame rose to devour the twisting form and turn it to delicate black ashes.

Remembrance of the Countryside

Nguyen Huy Thiep

I AM NHAM. I was born in a village and grew up in a village. If you're on Route 5 and looking toward my village, you'll only see a small green spot in the yellow fields. You can vaguely see the outline of the Dong Son Mountains, which seem close but are actually 50 kilometers away. My village is near the ocean, and in the summer an ocean breeze blows through.

The fifth month of the moon calendar is harvest time. My mother, my brother's wife, Ngu, Uncle Phung, and I are out in the fields by dawn. Those three cut, and I haul the rice.

I haul the rice home, following the edge of the path by the ditch. It's very bright outside, probably over 100°. The dry mud at the edge of the ditch is broken like rice crackers.

I'm very dreamy, always thinking. My father is a major in the navy, a middle-ranking technician who travels to many islands setting up radar instruments. Once a year he gets permission to come home. My father knows the names of all the islands by heart. My mother has never gone far from our village. She says, "Everywhere's the same. In every place, there are just people." Uncle Phung is different. He's been to a lot of places, and when he and I are alone together, he tells me, "Within the universe there are not only people, but also saints and devils." Uncle Phung's family is all women: his mother-in-law, his wife, and four daughters. Uncle Phung jokes: "I am the most handsome man in the family."

Ngu is my sister-in-law, married to my older brother Ky, who works in the Tinh Tuc iron mines in Cao Bang. Ngu is the daughter of Quy, the village elementary school teacher. I used to study with him. He has a lot of books. Everybody calls him "the eccentric scholar." They also say, "He's an old goat," and "Quy, the goat." Teacher Quy has two wives. The first wife gave birth to Ngu, my sister-in-law, and the second, Aunt Nhung, who both sews and keeps a small shop, is the mother of my friend Van. Aunt Nhung used to be a prostitute in Hai Phong. After Quy married her, there was nothing left of his reputation.

I haul ten loads of rice, which fill the courtyard. Then I call Minh to pile the straw to make room for the rice. Minh is my little sister, skinny and dark, but bright-eyed and tough. She comes out of the kitchen, her face red, her clothes soaked with sweat.

I go out to the barrel of rainwater, fill a coconut shell, and drink it in a few gulps. The water is cool. My mother often eats rice with rainwater and salted eggplant. My mother can't eat fatty meat.

The courtyard is scorching, and it feels like the air is steaming, heavy with the smell of rice.

Rice husks lay haphazardly across the village paths. When I walk by Aunt Luu's gate I see a crowd of people. Aunt Luu's daughter Mi calls, "Nham!" The village postman, Ba Ven, is cramming letters and newspapers into the canvas bag on the back of his bicycle. Mi tells me, "We have a telegram from Quyen in Hanoi."

Aunt Luu, my mother's younger sister, has been paralyzed for years. Her husband, Uncle Sang, is a transportation engineer working in Laos. Uncle Sang's older brother in Hanoi has a daughter, Quyen, who's been studying at a university in America. She came to visit when she was a child.

I hold the telegram in my hand and read: "Aunt Luu send someone to come meet me at the station at two o'clock." I ask Mi, "This afternoon?" Mi nods her head.

Aunt Luu is lying with her back against the wall. She's been lying like that for the past six years. She says, "Nham, help me by going to meet Quyen at the station, okay?"

I say, "My family's harvesting the rice."

"Leave it for a while. Which plot are you harvesting?"

"Red Fetus Plot," I tell her.

Mi carries the telegram out to the fields to talk to my mother. Mi is the same age as my sister Minh, but lighter skinned and more solid. She talks a lot and demands a lot of attention. "Hey, Nham," she says. "One day will you make a bamboo picker so I can get some guavas?" You make it from fresh bamboo, with a head like a fish trap with open teeth.

I tell Minh, "You have to find the bamboo."

"I found it already. Do it tomorrow, okay?"

I calculate in my head the things I need to do, and see I'm going to be busy from early morning until late at night. Mi says, "Tomorrow."

I say, "Yeah." Her house has three guava trees. One time she climbed one of them and the branch broke and she just barely missed falling.

Uncle Phung reads the telegram and says, "What's this SNN post office? What does it mean?"

My mother says, "Nham, if Aunt Luu asked you to go, then go. I put your new shirt in the trunk. Take it out and wear it."

I tell Mi, "Go home. I have to cut rice until noon. I'll go right after lunch."

Mi goes home alone. Her shadow sinks little by little into the field, which is rough with the stubble of the just-cut rice. I hold the sickle, gather the rice in an arc around me close to the roots, and pull sharply. I go one step to the left, gather again, and pull sharply. Go one step to the left again, gather again, and pull sharply again. Like that. Like that forever. The earth in the field is wet, and you can hear the tick tack sound of tiny grasshoppers dancing.

By noon, the fields are empty. Looking out I can see only the four people in my own family still out in the fields. My mother sits at the edge, pulling thorns from her foot. Ngu, wearing a conical hat, a scarf over her face, and with her legs wrapped from the ankles to the thighs for protection, is looking dreamily toward the far row of the Dong Son Mountains. Uncle Phung is collecting rice to haul home. He says, "Are you going home now?" My mouth is so dry I can't speak, so I only nod my head. The two of us, each with one load, head home. Uncle Phung goes in front, and I go behind. The loads of rice are heavy. My feet are shaking but I try to walk anyway. One hundred steps. Two hundred steps. One thousand steps. Two thousand steps. Like that. Like that forever. Then we get home.

Minh sets out my lunch and then hurries to carry it out to the field for my mother and Ngu.

Lunch is rice with boiled vegetables, salted eggplant, and preserved fish. I eat six bowls of rice without stopping. Now I'm tired. If not, I would eat a lot more.

I go out to the well to wash and change my clothes. I take out the new shirt and put it on, but I feel self-conscious and have to stop. I end up putting on my father's faded shirt from the army instead. Then I walk over to Aunt Luu's house to get the bicycle. Aunt Luu says, "Take a little money." She hands me five thousand but I only take two. Two thousand is worth more than a kilo of rice. Aunt Luu asks, "Do you remember Quyen's face?" I nod, though actually I don't remember well, but when I meet her I'll recognize her.

I ride the bicycle to the station. From my village to the station is four or five miles. It's been a long time since I've gone that far.

The dirt path follows the edge of the village past the village meeting house, past the lotus pond, then along the side of a ditch back toward the town hall. I'm thinking. But my ideas aren't clear.

I'm thinking
I'm thinking about the simplicity of words
Forms of expression are too powerless
While exhaustion fills the world
Shameless injustice fills the world

Desolate fates fill the world
How many months pass by
How many lives pass by
No word has the skill to describe it
Who will gather this morning for me
Gather the empty light from my little sister's eyes
Gather the gray hairs from my mother's head
Gather the vain hopes from the heart of my brother's wife
And gather the smell of poverty from the countryside
I snipe at every idea
I look for a way to chase it into a cage
And I scream in the fields of my heart
Howl like a wolf
I try to harvest some part of a life
And tie it loosely with a band of words
I howl in the fields of the body
I gather the light from the eyes of life
Which are watching the light in my own eyes
Looking into the world of consciousness
The distant and immeasurable world of consciousness
Although I understand
It means nothing, nothing, nothing, nothing, nothing at all.

The train station is empty in the afternoon. A few chickens stand in the courtyard. About ten people are waiting at the entrance. There's the sound of music coming from a cassette somewhere. The voice of the singer Nha Phuong slowly sings: "You passed through my life. Do you remember anything? My darling, you passed through my life. Do you remember anything?" Noodle soup vendors, refreshment vendors. Everywhere there are shops selling clothes, shoes, sugar and milk, cigarettes. Cars running back and forth.

The sky is so clear. Blazing. The whole town has sunstroke.

The train's whistle sounds hesitant and happy from far away. Someone calls, "The train's coming." The whole town is still dreamy. Then someone yells again, "The train's coming," and now the train sounds intimidating and shrill. Everybody's suddenly excited. Old women, young women, children selling things, all running back and forth. The sound of the sellers competing with each other. "Water, here!" "Bread!" "Drinks!" "Bread!" "Drinks!"

I stand with my bicycle, watching. The passengers are standing and sitting in a group at the doors of the train. This is a local stop. My countryside is anonymous. The place where I stand is anonymous.

About ten people file, one after another, through the ticket entrance, and I recognize a few teachers from the district high school. A soldier. A few traders. Some steelworkers. A fat man wearing dark glasses with the price sticker still on them. A tall, thin youth, with hair as brittle as the roots of bamboo and intense eyes. I know him. He's the poet Van Ngoc. After Ngoc comes an old couple. Quyen.

Quyen's hair hangs down. She wears a T-shirt, jeans, glasses, and a bag over her shoulder. Next to everyone else, Quyen stands out.

She walks through the ticket gate and looks around. She recognizes me immediately. "I'm Quyen," she says. "Did Aunt Luu send you to pick me up?"

"Yes," I say.

Quyen smiles. "Thank you. How are you related to Aunt Luu? What's your name?"

"I'm Nham. I'm the son of Hung."

"Do we share any common ancestors?"

"No."

Quyen nods. "Good. Aunt Luu hired you then?"

I look at my shadow, dark in the cement, my heart sad. Me, it's my destiny; everywhere people always see me as someone for hire.

The afternoon passes slowly. Shadows chase each other across the ground. The afternoon empties the spirit of anyone who hopes to prove that anything has meaning.

Quyen asks, "How many *sao* does your family plant? One *sao* harvests how much rice? How much money do you make?"

I tell her, "Every *sao* harvests more than a hundred kilos. Every kilo of rice sells for 1400 *dong*."

Quyen calculates. "Twenty million tons of rice for sixty million people."

I say, "Who only thinks about eating?"

Passing the lotus pond we meet Thieu, the monk. Brother Thieu says hello. I say hello back. Brother Thieu says, "I remembered to set aside some *tu cau* roses for you."

I say, "I'd like to come by the pagoda to get them sometime." I love flowers. Teacher Quy always says, "That's the pleasure of a person who understands life."

Brother Thieu asks, "Want to take a few lotus flowers to put in a vase?" This season the pagoda's lotus pond has a lot of flowers.

I park the bike to push the boat out for Brother Thieu. The basket boat can hold only one person sitting down. The paddle splashes the water. Quyen says, "I want to go on the boat." So I call Brother Thieu, and he rows back to shore.

Brother Thieu carries a bunch of lotus flowers up to the bank. Quyen climbs into the boat, and I push it back out with her in it.

Brother Thieu says, "Pampering people brings trouble to us." I laugh. He and I sit on the bank. The afternoon continues to pass slowly. Bright yellow sunshine. My heart is empty and wide, so empty, an empty expanse.

Quyen comes up the bank, and Brother Thieu invites us to eat lotus root. "Is it good?" he asks.

"It's good," she says.

We linger a little and then go home. Brother Thieu says good-bye. Quyen says good-bye back. Quyen carries the bunch of lotus flowers. Brother Thieu looks hesitantly after us for a moment.

I go in front. Quyen goes behind. She asks me about Brother Thieu.

THE STORY OF BROTHER THIEU

Brother Thieu was an orphan. In his fifteenth year someone looked at his strange physiognomy and told him, "You must go into the monkhood. There's no place in this world to hold you." Brother Thieu followed this advice; then he traveled to many different places, seeking to learn from great intellectuals, but he never got a chance. Brother Thieu said, "Now Buddha is living in a place that has no Buddha." Then he said: "Religion that's not intellectualized suits people; people who don't intellectualize are suited to religion."

Brother Thieu discovered the foundation of an old pagoda, then he mobilized the community's resources to help restore it. Inexplicably, it was called Bach Xi Tu, White Tooth Pagoda. Brother Thieu often read poetry. One poem was a couplet in the old language:

> *Co luan doc chieu giang son tinh*
> *Tu tieu nhat thinh thien dia kinh*

which means:

> *Only one orbit of light,*
>   *the mountain and river are quiet.*
> *Only one surge of laughter,*
>   *earth and heaven are afraid.*

There was another:

> *Lo phung kiem khach tu trinh kiem*
> *Bat thi thi nhan mac hien thi*

which means:

> *If you meet a swordsman, show your sword.*
> *If you're not a poet, don't chant your poetry.*

Brother Thieu said, "Buddha teaches humanity one way of entering the monkhood practically, by trying to rediscover one's original character. Buddha is too simple, so not everyone understands."

Quyen and I get home. Aunt Luu, with her eyes full of tears, cries, "Niece! Oh, niece!"

Quyen sits on the edge of the bed and says, "My mother and father remembered the anniversary of Grandfather's death, but they're busy and can't come. They sent you and Uncle a little money."

Aunt Luu says, "We don't need money. We only need feeling."

Quyen takes five million *dong* out of her purse and gives it to Aunt Luu. Quyen says, "I'm giving Mi a shirt."

Mi smiles shyly. "Thank you," she says.

I tell Aunt Luu, "I'm going home." Then I stuff her two thousand *dong* under her pillow and leave.

At home they're husking the rice. Ngu asks, "Is little Quyen pretty?"

"Yes," I tell her.

By the time dinner is over, it's dark. Outside, it's pouring. Thunder resounds in the sky. My whole family runs around pulling the rice out from under the leaks in the rafters. By the time we've finished it's already 11:00. It's still raining. Suddenly I feel anxious and can't sit still. I say to my mother, "I want to go out to the fields to catch frogs. In a rain like this there'll be a lot of frogs."

My mother says, "You're not afraid of the thunder and lightning, child?" I laugh. My mother doesn't understand my laugh at all. I laugh like a bandit, like a debt collector, like a devil. I laugh at my fingernails and toenails. Why are they so long and black like that?

SONG FOR CATCHING FROGS

The souls of the frogs return
I lie in dry ground, now I hop to the field's edge
Where there are only holes and burrows
No blankets, no mats; misery in a hundred forms
I pray for March to come.
With one big rain I can leap outside
Outside is so spacious and relaxed
In rain or sun I can always look for food
Before, I still strove to improve myself.
Unsuccessful, I was humbled.
I see a boy with nearly black skin
He just stands and looks without speaking
I see a boy with very black skin
In one hand a fishing rod, in the other, a basket.
He wears a conical hat
With a scarf wrapped around his head looking pretty
He also carries a fan
He carries a bamboo cylinder full of bait
He carries a slender rod
With a long red line.
I just sat down at the edge of the sweet potato field
He jerks his rod and breaks my jaw
Mother! Get me medicine
Get me the leaves of chili and xuong song *herbs*
I am in the deepest hole
At the edge of the morning glory pond near the raft.
Bamboo Shoot Boy is the son of Uncle Bamboo Tree
He catches me to take home to dry and skin.
The Welsh Onion Boy goes with the Flowering Onion Boy

Add a fistful of salt, so hot, so bitter.
Oh, Buddha, come down to me
Gather the martyred soul of this frog and fly back to heaven
A lifetime mixes tears and laughter
A frog's life, a person's life, so hot, so bitter . . .

The fields are empty. Only the sound of frogs croaking, the sound of toads echoing loudly, and the murmur of insects.

It rains.

It rains continuously.

I hold the flashlight, my feet treading randomly on the wet rice stubble. There are a lot of frogs, stunned by the light, and you only need to pick them up and put them in the basket. Thunder resounds in the sky. Lightning flashes. The universe opens without limits. The wind roars, sounding like thousands of birds flapping their wings over my head. Suddenly my soul is seized by a feeling of terror. Very clearly, I see a great image gliding quickly and moving violently over my head. I lie down on the ground, stupefied, gasping. I feel certain that the invisible power hovering above me understands everything absolutely, justly, clearly, defending the inherent goodness of the human soul. It has the ability to comfort and soothe each person's fate. It brings me peace.

I was right
I am at peace because I chose this form of expression
The form is difficult, mediocre, meaningless, and vain
To add luster to the value of human knowledge
In these deserted fields
The deserted fields of stupidity and defiant cruelty

Who's there?
Who plays the plaintive flute at night?
And which bright souls, which dark souls are searching
  for the way
Which faint breath
Which faint laughter
Emerges screeching out of white teeth
Which whispers
Meaningless groans of insects
Sounds of the cowherd's flute, which are tiny but carry
Wandering through the fields of the heart
Wandering through the fields of the body
Which wanderer survives
Which soulmates listen closely
Which origins remind
Strumming musical sounds
On this dark night who remains awake
Who wanders through the fields of this immense and
  miserable world?

Little by little the rain stops. I go around this field, around that field. The big croakers have disappeared. Sometimes I can only see one peeper running along the canal. On the horizon, in the direction of Dong Son, I see the flicker of a fire. I feel lost. I don't know what time it is but suddenly I hear the crow of the chickens, the desolate crow of the chickens falling and rising in no order at all. For a long time I don't see any frogs, then suddenly I realize that somehow I've come to the place where the canal meets the Cam River. Alone in the sky is the morning star.

It's dawn when I return to the village. The air is clean.

The village is familiar and quiet. After the rain, the land-scape seems elegant and pure.

Crossing by Aunt Nhung's house, I stand still. The house is situated close to the side of the road. The thatch screen opens. Someone's shadow slips hurriedly out. Who-ever it is looks in front and behind then runs quickly and hides behind a tree. A thief? I'm about to yell when I re-alize it's Uncle Phung. A moment later, Aunt Nhung opens the door and steps tranquilly out, wearing a night-gown. Nhung is over thirty, her body well proportioned and beautiful.

I carry the bag of frogs down the road after Uncle Phung. When we get to a bend, he glances back and sees me. He says, "Were there many frogs?" I don't answer. Uncle Phung is a bit startled. He insists, "Why are you being like that?" I suddenly feel a gnawing sadness. I'm sad for Aunt Nhung, sad for Uncle Phung, sad for Teacher Quy. I'm sad for myself.

Uncle Phung walks away as if he doesn't care. I go home. It turns out that I only have about twenty frogs. Ngu says, "That wasn't worth the effort. So few and you were out all night."

My mother laughs, "He probably caught frogs and slept in the fields."

Minh is preparing to go to school for the summer ac-tivities. She wears blue pants and a white blouse, which are her nicest clothes, the ones she only wears on holi-days. She whispers in my ear, "I know where you went, but I won't tell. You didn't go catch frogs." She laughs. I look into her eyes. She *knows*, but I have no way to sus-pect that in only a few hours I will have to cry for her. She *knows*, simply because it's almost like she's experienced things and understands. Until that moment, the moment when she will die, she has only four more hours to joke and understand everything completely.

My mother says, "Child, take some frogs over to Teacher Quy's so he can drink whiskey with them."

I say, "Okay," then I go bathe.

My mother and Ngu go out to the fields to harvest peanuts, which is also my job in the mornings.

On the way to Teacher Quy's house, I go by Aunt Luu's, and Quyen yells, "Hey, What's-your-name!"

I say, "I'm Nham. Where did Mi go?"

"Mi went to school. Wherever you're going, let me go with you."

We go to Teacher Quy's.

THE STORY OF TEACHER QUY

Teacher Quy taught elementary school, had a generous nature, and had been reading books since he was small. When he grew up and his parents chose a wife for him, he said to her, "Don't marry me or you'll have a miserable life."

She said, "Even miserable, I'll still marry you."

Teacher Quy said, "If you marry me, first, you can't be afraid of poverty; second, you can't be afraid of humiliation; third, you can't be jealous; and fourth, you have to respect decency."

She said, "If you respect decency, then the other three are easy." The couple got married and lived in harmony.

Later, Teacher Quy lost his job because he couldn't bear to follow the textbooks and taught with proverbs and popular songs instead. One time he went to Hai Phong to administer a test and he met a pregnant prostitute who had no place to deliver her baby, so he brought her home to be his second wife. The first wife didn't say anything, even contributed money to build another house. Wife number two wasn't faithful, and still had relationships with a lot of men, but Teacher Quy ignored it. He only said, "Whoever you sleep with, remember to get some money out of him. If there's no money, then take rice, or a pig or a duck. Don't sleep with someone for nothing." The whole village laughed at him, but Teacher Quy ignored them. Teacher Quy often drank whiskey. Whiskey went in, and poetry came out. There were a lot of poems that were pretty good.

Teacher Quy is at home by himself, lying on a hammock reading a book. Quyen and I say hello. He gets up and hurries to make tea. We sit on a bamboo bed under the shade of the vine trellis. The teacher asks Quyen, "Miss, if you study at the university in America, who is it useful for?"

Quyen says, "It's useful for me, useful for my family, useful for the country."

Teacher Quy smiles. "Don't think about usefulness. It'll only exhaust you."

We eat taro dipped in sesame and salt. When Teacher Quy shoves a book under the mat, Quyen says, "If you do that, you'll crush the book and ruin it."

Teacher Quy laughs. "If I crush it, it's nothing. You

read books to have knowledge. Having knowledge is for having a life with meaning."

The sunlight filters through the leaves, scattering traces of light on the ground. Teacher Quy and Quyen and I are quiet. I want to go out into the fields. Quyen says, "Coming back this time, I really want to have an accurate impression of the countryside. Wherever you go, let me go with you." I hesitate.

Teacher Quy laughs, "She's a woman. How can you refuse a woman?"

We say good-bye to Teacher Quy and go into the fields. Quyen says, "The fields are so wide. Do you know where they begin?"

The fields began in a place very deep in my heart
Within my own flesh and blood there were fields
From over here, the fields were immense and limitless
From over there, the fields were limitless and immense
How can I ever forget the place where my mother gave birth
*   to me*
Where she used thread to cinch the stem of my umbilical cord
Washed me in pond water
I knew that crying was useless because everything must wait
Must wait from January to December
In January plant beans; in February, eggplant
I have passed along so many wrong paths
I have passed through so many hardships, vulgarities
I must plant and harvest in this field
I must know by heart the names of so many kinds of bugs
And the field is sometimes rainy, sometimes sunny
Some places are shallowly raked and some are deeply plowed

Then one day
(an inauspicious and ominous day)
A woman came and made me miserable
She taught me the custom of unfaithfulness in love
By betraying me as she would betray anyone
I silently buried my hatred at the end of the fields
In a difficult vein of the fields, shaped like the curve of a
*   sword*
Flowers of hope withered in my hand
Work became heavier than before
I sold produce at a price too cheap
I have had several big harvests
And also failed completely several times
When the afternoon passed, twilight was quiet
I had no time to see the scars on my body
I only knew that I was wounded
Night
The stars burned like candles in the sky
I covered myself with a shroud, which smelled of my comrade
At that moment, Oh, Friend, Oh my young friend
Please understand me
I tried to make the fields so fertile

I lead Quyen past the auxiliary crops. She asks, "How much has the local price for agricultural products changed this year?"

"It's gone up 0.4 percent," I tell her.

"That'll kill you! Industrial products rose 2.2 percent," she says. "What's the price of fertilizer?"

"Nitrogen increased 1.6 percent. Phosphorus increased 1.4 percent."

"Do you use electricity here?" she asks.

"No."

"The price of electricity rose 2.2 percent."

Around ten o'clock in the morning the fields get crowded with women and children. They're the main source of labor. The men around here are adventurous. They have a lot of illusions and nurse dreams of getting rich, so they often take off for the city to look for work or to do business. There are even some people who risk going as far as the center of the country to dig for gold or rubies. They don't strike it rich, but when they return to the village, their characters have changed. They've become like wild and dangerous beasts. Uncle Phung is a person like that.

THE STORY OF UNCLE PHUNG

Nguyen Viet Phung, the child of a poor family, went through secondary school and then quit. Phung had a number of professions: plowman, builder, carpenter, ox-cart driver. When he was twenty he went into the army. Three years later he returned to the village and got married. His wife, who is four years older than he is, gave birth to four girls in three years (two are twins). Phung was determined to get rich, so he sold all the furniture in his house for two gold rings, which he carried to the center of the country to dig for gold. For a year, there was no news at all, and then out of nowhere he returned, thin as the corpse of a cicada, his face swollen like a gong. He lay down on the bed and his hardworking wife had to take care of him for the next six months. The poor family became poorer. After his battle with illness, Phung's manner changed. Once he stabbed someone, scaring everyone in the village. Another time he suddenly started crying, putting his hands together in prayer and prostrating himself before his wife and daughters. Luckily, after that, his wife's parents moved to the city to live with their son who had just returned from abroad. They gave the family the house with three *sao* of land and that changed their lives. Phung's wife is resourceful, good at raising animals, and also at making and selling tofu. Every one of those four daughters endures a lot to help her mother. At home, Phung has one room for himself, which he forbids his wife and children to enter. Sometimes he still goes with Nhung and a few of the local matrons. Phung's wife and daughters ask, "Why do you avoid us?" Phung says, "There's nothing valuable that's close to me. My flesh is poison. Biting me would poison a dog. I love all of you. All I want is for you to be clean."

Quyen and I pass a peck of land in the middle of the fields. At the bottom, castor-oil plants and thorny amaranth grow abundantly. There is even corn with red flowers and green leaves. Quyen asks, "Why is it called a 'peck' of land?"

"In the past, King Ba Vanh dug this pit as a space in which to count the number of soldiers he had, in the same way that we would measure rice."

"About how many people?"

"Twenty people would be one fighting unit and two hundred people would be one battalion."

Quyen and I reach the field where my mother and Ngu

are gathering peanuts. Water fills the plot, prompting the peanut plants to rise from their roots.

Quyen rolls up her trousers and wanders down to collect peanuts. "It's so easy," she says.

My mother says, "You're only here for a short time. Try to calculate from the moment we first sow peanut seeds into the furrows until we harvest, then you might understand how muddy and exhausted my children and I can be."

Ngu adds, "Whoever has a full bowl of rice should remember that each grain is full of bitterness."

I step into a nest of crickets. When I turn the ground with a shovel, thousands of big, fat ones swarm into the air. My mother and Ngu stop gathering peanuts to catch crickets. My mother, grinning with pleasure, says, "Oh, a blessing! Such abundance for our family! Oh!"

Ngu says happily, "Maybe our family will be the richest in the village!"

About noon, we see on Route 5 a group of people screaming and crying and running around. My mother falls headfirst into the field, then calls to me, "Nham! Oh, Nham!" Ngu and I are afraid, thinking my mother has been blown over by the wind. My mother's face grows pale, and she puts her hands in front of her as if she's touching somebody, saying, "Nham! Oh, Nham! Why does your sister Minh have blood all over her face like that?"

Ngu shakes my mother, "Mother! Mother! Why are you talking like that?"

A few people suddenly separate from the crowd on Route 5 and run across the fields. Someone screams loudly and sorrowfully, "Mrs. Hung (Hung is my father's name), hurry and get the body of your child." Ngoc (the poet I saw at the station yesterday afternoon), with his hair standing on end, runs in the lead. He doesn't speak clearly. I only hear it vaguely, only hear enough to know that my little sister Minh and Aunt Luu's daughter Mi were riding through the three-way intersection on their way home from school when a truck carrying electric posts hit and killed them.

My mother writhes in the peanut field, smearing herself with dirt. The crickets skip up off the ground, fly for a moment, then drop back down to bury their heads in the mud. Ngu stands silently, her eyes confused and full of fear, looking off in the direction of the Dong Son Mountains as if she can't understand why the heavens suddenly became so cruel.

Ngoc, Quyen, and I run out to the road. Tears are streaming down my face. Minh was only thirteen years old. Mi was only thirteen years old. I hadn't even had a chance to make the guava picker for Mi. And my little sister, Minh, a child so generous she wore only patched clothes her whole life and always set aside for me the most delicious things to eat.

The truck carrying three electric posts lies turned over by the edge of the road. People are using a jack to raise the wheel, looking for a way to pull out the bodies of Minh and Mi. Minh lies on her side, Mi on her stomach, pressed against each other, with the crumpled bicycle next to them.

I put my hand to my mouth to stifle any cries. I loved them so much. Swarms of flies cluster around their noses. I don't know where Ngoc got the handful of incense he's now holding in front of the faces of the two girls. The smoke lingers in one place, unable to rise.

I won't say anything else about the deaths of Minh and Mi. In the afternoon we have to have the funeral for my sister and my cousin. It's like every other funeral in the village, with lots of tears, lots of condolences. One of the village youths and I carry Aunt Luu on a stretcher out to the end of the fields and then later carry her back. Quyen follows. Ngoc wrote a poem about the whole thing. I don't understand how he could write a poem during such a brutal time as this.

THE FUNERAL OF THE VIRGINS IN THE FIELDS
BY THE POET BUI BAN NGOC

I follow the funeral of the virgins into the fields
White death, completely white death
White butterflies, white flowers
White souls, white lives
Oh, I follow the funeral of the virgins into the fields
I dig a grave, five feet long, two feet wide
I dig a grave, four feet deep
Oh, I bury these spirits that were only beginning
Oh, here is an offering for the earth
Completely pure virgins, completely white death
White butterflies, white flowers
White spirits, white lives
Oh, I stow in my heart this pure white poem
I break off a green branch to cover my eyes
The breeze flutters, the spirit flutters away

The spirit flies away, over the fields of the body
I follow the funeral of the virgins into the field
On a day like that, not a special day
On a day like that, a normal day
Oh, I am lost in the crowd, in the masses, in the hearts,
   in the grief, in the desolation. . . .

The next afternoon, I take Quyen to the station. Aunt Luu cries forever, but Quyen insists on leaving. We follow the dirt road that runs along the edge of the village. At the lotus pond we sit down to rest. Quyen says, "I've only been here three days, but it seems so long!"

In the afternoon the district station is empty. There are only about ten people standing in the yard waiting for the train. In the emptiness you can hear sounds coming from a cassette player somewhere. The train arrives. One by one the passengers get on the train. Some teachers from the district high school. A soldier. A few traders. A teenager wearing clear glasses, carrying a suitcase. An old couple. Quyen.

Quyen says, "Hey! What's-your-name! I'm leaving! Thanks for coming to the station with me!"

I stand in the station yard for a long time. The train disappears. I have a feeling I'll never see Quyen again.

I pass through the ticket gate and go back to the village. From the side, you can only see a small green spot in the yellow fields and vaguely, in the distance, the outline of the Dong Son Mountains. I have so many remembrances there.

Will tomorrow be sunny or rainy? Actually, rain and sunshine are both meaningless to me now. I am Nham. Tomorrow I will be seventeen years old. Is that the most beautiful time in a person's life or not?

Translated by Dana Sachs and Nguyen Van Khang

The Colonel

Thich Duc Thien

IN FRONT of my refreshment stand, on the other side of the street, a colonel used to squat under the *sau* tree. He patched and pumped tires for a living. I didn't know how long he'd been there, or where he came from. These days, there are a lot of people pumping tires for a living. No one paid attention to him.

Some of my customers kept saying, "He's a colonel." But no one was surprised, for there's the saying:

> *At one end of the village, a colonel pumps tires.*
> *At the other, a brigadier sells black bean pudding.*

One night, while watching TV, my children yelled out, "Oh, it's the tire-pumping colonel."

It was, indeed, the colonel on the TV. He was celebrating some historic victory. He wore the three stars of a colonel and a lot of medals. Why did he have to pump tires? Something was not quite right here, but these days (as before) heroes fallen on hard times are common. This was why I, like everyone else, didn't care.

One day, some French visitors were looking for a street, fumbling with a map, confused. The colonel spoke

French fluently, and showed them the way. They were thrilled and shook his hand, twittering like birds. I couldn't understand them but could tell that they were thanking him.

It was because of that incident that I had the occasion to invite him into our home. I asked him to translate a letter my younger siblings had sent from Switzerland, written in French. In the year of the famine, my mother and I were begging around. After she sold me, my mother disappeared. One day, the local chapter of the Red Cross passed on to me a letter from Switzerland. My mother had been brought to Switzerland by a Spaniard in the French Foreign Legion, and both became naturalized there. After he and my mother passed away, their children—my younger siblings—asked for help from the Red Cross and found my address. From then on, I regularly received their letters and dollars. The only trouble was none of my siblings knew Vietnamese, and all their letters were in French. I had to go hire someone to translate them, thirty thousand *dong* a page. I didn't mind the money, but it always took a lot of time. My luck was finding the colonel. I no longer had to struggle. My siblings asked about our home village in their letters, someplace in the old province of Ha Dong, either Do or Dó or Dỏ, but since French language has no tone marks, it was difficult to tell. I had been moving about since I was a child; I couldn't tell what village that was.

I tried to give the old man a fee for the translation, but he didn't want it. I offered him some 555 cigarettes, but he declined, saying he had quit smoking. When I offered beer, coffee, tea, he also shook his head, claiming that he had stomach trouble and had to refrain from any stimulants. I told him, "When my brothers and sisters visit, I must insist on inviting you to celebrate with us, and to help translate for us at the same time."

Since then, he became a relative in my mind, even an important family member, though he was just pumping tires all day long under the *sau* tree.

Some time later he disappeared, and I became worried. Was he sick? Where could I visit him? One night, after returning from a wedding in our neighborhood, I was shocked to hear the news from my children. "The Colonel is dead," they said. They had seen an obituary on TV. I asked them, "Where was he buried?"

"We didn't pay attention."

I scolded them for being heartless. But these days the young are generally that heartless.

I don't remember how many days passed, but soon after I received a letter from him. I didn't know who had sent it. He was very succinct, but the handwriting was wobbly, proof that the writer was ill.

> I found your home village. It's the village of Đo', not Do or Dó. It is now the hamlet of . . . in the district of . . . in the province of Ha Tay. It's my home village, too. Not only are we from the same village, we are actually related, on your father's side. You are above me in familial rank. I should have given you the good news long ago, but I was quite afraid. Please understand, but I was afraid your wife and children or your neighbors might suspect that this tattered old tire-pumper was just trying to claim a

relationship to rich folks. That's why I asked my
family not to send this letter until I passed away.
Please forgive me.

He had signed the letter, but the signature was illegible.

Translated by Nguyen Qui Duc

How Long until the End of Bitterness?

Vu Bao

EVEN WITH THE WOOL blanket pulled over her neck, Luu was still feeling the coldness of the mat against her cheek, her shoulder, her palm, her legs, penetrating all the way to her ribs, and inside her heels. Try as she might to turn to all corners of her bed, she couldn't avoid the cold and dampness, so Luu had to lie on her side, blocking herself in with the corners of her blanket, trapping just her own human heat to warm herself.

Things that seemed buried in the months and years were now crowding back. Luu closed her eyes but could not chase them away. Heavens, who could fight off the kind of coldness that comes from inside the soul? How long will suffering cling to a woman's fate?

Thirty years before, the whole of the Che region was able to cultivate only a little rice. On that plain, shaped like a deep frying pan, as early as January, villagers were already having to build roads to carry water back for their rice stalks, but by May, they had to work under water. There were some bad rains, and the mud roads all collapsed. Soon, water from far away was flooding and turning the field white, and people visiting neighboring villages had to use sampans to travel. During such months of voluminous water, main roads and paths were all flooded, and people fetching kindling to the villages had to use banana trunks to travel on the water. The elders used to say, "Six months out of the year, Che villagers walk with their hands."

On the latest market day, a woman living in Dan Phuong sent a message asking Mr. Tiu and his wife to come pick up a basket of yams to carry them through the difficult days. Mr. Tiu's wife was so glad. They had a sampan, but Mr. Tiu had taken it to go work in the mines, so Mrs. Tiu borrowed a neighbor's dinghy to row over to Phung market.

When she set out, there was a slight wind. Halfway, the wind picked up, and there were powerful waves. Each time Mrs. Tiu wrenched herself to maneuver the oars the dinghy would mount just a couple of waves and then twist itself around like a calf protesting its owner's pulls.

There were moments when Mrs. Tiu wanted to turn around to go home, but she thought about the effort it would take and knew it would be just the same to continue on to market to fetch the basket of yams. The wind was scraping the surface of the water, sounding like strips of fabric being torn. Mrs. Tiu felt the pain in her stomach again. She was pregnant with her first child, but she was sure it was just a shiver from the wind and forced herself to row. Moments later, she became feverish and felt as if someone were reaching inside her stomach, yanking at different parts of her intestines. She had to sit on the bottom of the dinghy, holding her belly with one hand, the oar with the other. When she could no longer withstand the pain, she collapsed, unaware that the oars had fallen into the water.

The dinghy floated around on the water. The waves threw in bursts of water, soaking her shirt. She thrashed about in pain.

An eagle spread its wings on the sky, contemplating the prey on the water. Its sharp eyes had caught the moving shadow in the spiraling boat. At first, Mrs. Tiu could see it just as a grain of rice in the sky. Later, while she was still thrashing at the bottom of the dinghy, she could see it just yards above her. Its wings were as big as banana leaves, its eyes were focused on her, and its sharp talons were extended.

Mrs. Tiu reached for a bailing can and waited until the eagle flapped its wings to dive down. Then she tried to hit the eagle's head with the can, forcing it to fly up to avoid the blow. A wind blew through, smelling like sewer water, and made her want to throw up. The eagle had retreated a good distance, perhaps realizing that the shadow in the dinghy was still alive rather than a floating corpse.

With sweat breaking out on her forehead, her hair sticking to her cheek and neck, Mrs. Tiu tried to call out, "Please help me. Somebody help me," but her depleted voice could not reach the banks. She felt a massive pain as if she were being torn in half, and grasped the side of the boat. The bamboo branches tied alongside the dinghy were squeezed together, making scraping noises.

Mrs. Tiu passed out. When she came to, she heard in the sound of the water slapping against the dinghy the cries of an infant. A foul and fishy odor came to her nose, mixed with the stench of wet, rotten bamboo and foul field water. She pushed herself against the side of the dinghy, took quick gulps of air, and saw a frightening pool of red water at the bottom of the boat. She gathered all her strength and reached for the baby squirming between her legs.

The dinghy floated about for a while until it banged against a raft. A man from the raft jumped into the water and pulled the dinghy to shore. He built a fire to warm mother and child and heated a knife to cut the umbilical cord. Villagers heard about the birth and summoned people to bring some old clothes for Mrs. Tiu and some scarves to cover the baby. They cooked a pot of rice and made hard-boiled eggs, feeding Mrs. Tiu to help her regain some strength. A woman with an infant of her own fed the newborn from her breast.

The next morning, the man with the raft took Mrs. Tiu and her child back to the village of Che on a boat.

Mrs. Tiu couldn't remember which village she had given birth in, but knew that the raft was from the Luu Xa camp and so named her daughter Luu. This way, when she was grown, the child would know where to go and offer gratitude to repay the debt to those who had saved her and her mother's life. The child's full name was Luu Thi Do.

The next year, Mr. Tiu fulfilled his citizens' labor duties, carrying rice up to Hoa Binh for the soldiers preparing a campaign in the lowlands, but the labor group got lost, arriving at the rice depot near morning. They set about to cook a meal. Reconnaissance aircraft discovered the smoke over the treetops and called in attack planes. Mr. Tiu died during the strike. Mrs. Tiu married into the Pham family to survive. After that, all of Luu's papers carried the last name Pham.

At eighteen, Luu married a man with the last name of Tran, before he joined the army. The couple lived with each other for three days, plus two days of rest after an attack, and the fifteen days of leave he had before going to the battlefields of Area B. Twenty days with a husband and a son-to-be. That was all the nineteen-year-old wife was to know of family happiness. Luu's husband was sent to battlefields far away and only once was able to send a letter home when he ran across a villager on a mission. She named her son Nam, South, to honor a husband who had gone to liberate the South and who would never get to see his son, even once, just for a short moment.

Of the ten villagers who went to Area B that time, no one had come back yet to tell her how her husband had died. In his last moments, what message had he wanted to send her? No one from his unit wrote to tell her the time and date of his death, nor did anyone sketch a map of the area where he was buried. The South had been liberated for five years now, but she didn't know where to go to build a tomb or light incense for her husband. The certificate of recognition from the government merely said he "had sacrificed his life on the southern front." Luu had to opt for the date he'd left as the day to carry out the ceremony for the dead.

While she was with him, she treated him in a way that gave her no regrets today. Once, on the day she saw him off at the bus stop, they had sat in a corner of the waiting room together, and Luu's husband had put his arm around her back and pulled her close. Luu had turned all red and gently removed his arm.

Luu's husband turned to ask her, "Aren't you going to miss me?"

Luu answered, "Yes."

Luu's husband then asked, "If you do, then sit closer to me." Luu shook her head slightly.

"They're looking at us."

She wished she had pleased her husband that one time, but what did it matter. Now one is in a photo, the other sitting in front of the altar; their eyes meet, but how could Luu come closer to her husband? Death is the end. The dead suffer through terrible moments before they cross into another world, but the living have nothing but days and days of loneliness while living in this world full of people.

Recently, a man by the name of Dong had come to Luu. Like a bit of hot coal ash falling onto a stack of hay, this late love was warming the widow in her lonely days. He had asked Luu not to leave with her friends. "I have something I want to talk to you about," he said. Although fearing a thousand eyes, Luu found a way to stay behind, cleaning up the meeting room. She waited until everyone had left before she went to her tryst with Dong.

Luu wanted tonight's road to continue without ever ending. It's been a dozen years since she could feel the sweetness she'd felt when she had first fallen in love.

Dong kept silent next to her, neither holding her hand nor putting his arm around her as they walked. Once in a while she would step into a pothole, and their shoulders would touch, and once she even felt his chest. Luu wanted to stop right there, but her feet kept moving in

time with his. Luu wanted to accompany him all the way
to Mr. Dan's house, but when they reached the clump of
bamboo near the village pond, by the road that turned toward her house, Luu stopped. If Dong had asked her,
Luu would have continued her walk with him. The two
sank into the shadow of the bamboo.

Dong reached for Luu, "Are you going home?"

Just as Luu placed her hand into Dong's palm, a voice
called out, "Mother!"

Luu withdrew her hand and turned to see where her
son was standing.

Nam was still awake. He stood by the bridge on the
pond, calling out loudly, "Mother! How come you're so
late?"

All Luu could say to Dong was, "Please understand."
And without waiting for a reply, she stepped out from the
shadows.

Dong called out, "Luu, stay. I want to say something."

She loved Dong so. She turned to hold his hand.

Nam's voice echoed from the bridge. "Mother. I saw
you."

Luu abandoned Dong's hand. When she was young she
was afraid of her parents and now she was afraid of her
son. She didn't dare turn around but quickened her steps
into her garden.

Luu caressed her son's back. "Go wash your feet and
then go to bed. You've got to get up for school in the
morning."

Nam laughed. "It's Sunday tomorrow. Did you forget?"
Nam quietly scooped up some water and threw it onto
the roof. The male cat jumped off the female cat and ran
to one side of the tiled roof.

Luu grabbed the scoop. "Don't be mean."

Nam was upset. "But it's always biting our cat."

Children will always have reasons that adults must swallow without a word.

Luu brightened the lamp wick, turning the pages in her son's notebook to check his math homework. The figures danced in front of her eyes. She kept re-reading them and feared she was misreading.

She closed the notebook, raised her head to tell Nam, "Wash your hands and feet and go to bed."

"Are you going somewhere again?"

"I'm going to bed."

Luu knew that at that moment Dong was still waiting for her in the shadow of the bamboo clump but she had no way of persuading her son to go to bed before her. She had to climb into bed, let down the mosquito net, and crawl under the blanket.

Each time she moved, the son asked from his bed, "Where are you going, Mother?"

Luu rolled toward the wall, wrapping her blanket around her hand, which still felt warm. Her son's calls stopped her from reaching for what she wanted. What she thought she had forgotten was now brought back by the warmth in her hand. Desperate want, burning desire made her eyes bulge.

Some years ago, when her son was learning to walk, many men had come to her. Luu had thought that now that she had a son, she should stay with him, wait for him to grow older, and avoid situations in which there would be talk of my child, your child, our child. For ten years Luu had always been invited to sit on honored chairs. Luu had been designated to present reports in conferences on the Three Readinesses or The Three Efficiencies or Citizen and Army Total-Victory Congresses. Journalists interviewed her, took photographs of her. Luu still didn't want to take the next step, determined to play the role of the wife of a fallen hero. But now she'd grown terrified of her loneliness, of winter nights. Luu was pining for a warm arm around her back, but time could no longer wait. Those who came to her before were now all settled down. Those coming to her now were struck by her son's selfish, querying eyes.

The wind was blowing steadily. The female cat stuck her belly to the roof, calling out for the male.

Lying in her blanket, Luu did not hear the response from a male cat. Perhaps it had been so terrified by the water that it would never return.

Luu's body was burning. She had to throw off the blanket, sat up, but did not move her feet in search for her sandals for fear her son would hear.

She pushed the door lightly and walked out to the front yard.

She sensed somebody in the bamboo shadow still.

Luu crossed the yard.

"Mother!"

Luu's feet were heavy as if tied to stone.

Luu sighed and turned around, scooping some water from the cistern. She raised her head and drank the water. There was only cold water on a winter night that could help the heat burning each cell in the widow's body.

Luu had just placed the scoop on the cistern when her son appeared in front of her.

Translated by Nguyen Qui Duc

Dresses, Dresses

Linh Bao

IN THOSE DAYS the most prized piece of clothing in our family was a tunic made of dark silk "bestowed upon us by His Majesty, the Emperor." My father was a minor functionary at the time, a paper-shuffler, a pencil-pusher, really. And my mother was engaged in a kind of informal antique business. She also had a second occupation that was quite extraordinary: armed with a camera, she made occasional forays into the Imperial Palace where she took pictures of the Royal Highnesses and Court Ladies!

As I said, my mother was an antique dealer. It was a leisurely profession. She would dress nicely, impeccably in fact, and, after rubbing her hair with coconut oil until it glistened like a black mirror, she would carefully part it straight down the middle and do it up. When she was satisfied with her appearance she would go to call on the noble ladies. She would regale them with stories and gossip; the ladies, invariably delighted, would respond in kind. In the course of the conversation, my mother would take all the information she needed: who wanted to sell or buy what, when and for how much. Then all she had to do was summon our rickshaw man, make a few leisurely trips here and there, and everyone—buyer and seller alike —would be happy.

Some fifty-plus years ago, photography was still a great novelty, especially for the court ladies, those assorted imperial favorites who were not free to go into town and walk around like other mortals. The ladies loved and needed my mother. Imagine one of these creatures, a second- or third-rank consort who had not even seen the Emperor's "dragon face" in years, and who now owned, thanks to my mother's photographic hocus-pocus, a print that showed her sitting proudly on an elaborately carved chair with who else but His Majesty himself beside her, one arm around the high-backed chair as though he were tenderly embracing her shoulders. My mother was very clever with photomontage. The ladies paid dearly for her skill. Of course, cold cash meant nothing to these fading beauties who, from the time of their selection and introduction into the palace until advanced age, even death, might well remain virgins! Her photographs in some way assuaged the craving for fame and glory inculcated in the ladies when they were girls.

Among my mother's customers, unbelievable as it may sound, was the Empress Dowager herself! Her son, the Emperor, was still very young and was studying abroad. A widow, the Empress lived alone in her palace surrounded by retainers and luxuries, and she spent her days playing cards in the company of flatterers and sycophants. Though hardly destitute, she broke all records as a "borrower" of money, borrowing without paying back of course. Probably she considered it everyone's duty to serve her by supplying her with cash for her card games.

True, she never forgot to soften the blow of her avarice by telling people in the most cunning, veiled way that they would be more than repaid once the young Emperor returned. I don't know if my mother unwittingly became one of Her Imperial Majesty's victims, but even if we had known, as children we would have had absolutely no say in the matter.

At that time, each of my four sisters owned a heavy gold necklace, which often traveled a very definite route several times a month from our house to that of Mrs. X— a very rich ladies' pawnbroker in town. Whenever my mother got hold of a substantial amount of cash, she would bring the necklaces home and, lo and behold, an order would arrive from Her Majesty that she "wished to accept grateful loans" from one of her favorite subjects. Thereupon our four gold necklaces would take off again for the deep coffers of Mrs. X. At least the necklaces were fortunate in that their journeys were round-trip, while the money that arrived from pawning them went only one way. Once the money passed from my mother's hands to Her Majesty's, it disappeared—who knew where— without a trace.

This was not all. Once in a while, Her Majesty deigned to descend upon our modest dwelling in the suburbs. I use the word "modest" not to be delicate, but as a realistic description. Our house was a simple bamboo-and-thatch cottage, which stood smack in the middle of an immense cemetery, about two miles from Hue. My parents had the house built there upon doctor's orders. My father had weak lungs and needed to live in a place where there was plenty of fresh air and lots of pine trees. Our modest dwelling sheltered at various times many prized objects, from antique furniture to expensive jewelry and assorted bric-a-brac. Not that any of these items belonged to us. Their owners were court ladies out of cash, who left them with my mother in the hope that she would find buyers. Of course the ladies had the greatest confidence in my mother's discretion: They were willing to part with their treasures for a price, but only if they could save face as well. And my mother certainly lived up to their trust.

The steep, winding road that led to our cottage was flanked on both sides by groves of pines. Once in a while a guard of the imperial household, dressed in conical hat, red coat, and yellow leggings, would painfully haul a lacquered vermilion and gold rickshaw up our hill. Close on his heels would be two girls in their midteens, wearing headbands and tunics of a rich, flaming yellow, their black hair flapping about their shoulders. One girl always carried the Empress's chewing paraphernalia—a box of betel and areca nuts in one hand, a silver spittoon in the other—while the second girl clutched a fan made of enormous feathers. Once in a while this one would rush back to the rickshaw, raise the fan with both hands, and flap it into the vehicle. Then she would resume her place next to the first girl. That was how Her Imperial Majesty, the Empress Dowager, made her way from the Forbidden City to our humble abode, some two miles distant.

When she arrived, Her Majesty would install herself upon the mother-of-pearl-encrusted platform that occupied the exact center of our house. Her two attendants stood guard, one fanning her, the other filling her teacup. Thus ensconced, she would leisurely cast her eyes about the house, admiring whatever we had of value at the moment. Naturally, when Her Imperial Majesty left, a few of these objects would leave, following her back to the palace. As she departed, Her Majesty would bestow a few kindly words upon my mother: "Now, my good woman, do keep a record of these vases *we* are taking today. Also that bonsai with jade leaves and gold branches. You'll be paid handsomely, *we* assure you. And about that carved sofa with the mother-of-pearl designs, *we* would like to borrow it for a while. Tomorrow some men will come to bring it to the palace. . . ."

My mother could only agree and swallow her tears. We all knew that, just like those beautiful young virgins, once a prized object—be it porcelain vase or teak chair—was "introduced to the palace," its fate was clear: gone forever. And actually those inanimate beauties had an even worse fate than the imperial concubines, for once the ladies reached a certain age that rendered them no longer attractive to the august imperial eye, they were customarily allowed to return to their native villages, while those other precious objects, gaining more value with age, never came back.

And so, life went on. My father went to work at his office, shuffling papers day in and day out, while my mother sold antiques and concocted pictures for the ladies. We always suspected that most of what she managed to make never helped bring us up at all, but went to support Her Majesty's bad habits.

One day, whether Her Majesty's conscience suddenly bothered her or she became fearful that all her accumulated debts in this life would turn into something much more terrible in the next, as the Buddhist scriptures taught, whatever the reason (and we were never sure) Her Majesty began to lavish praise on my mother and proceeded to honor her by bestowing on her and my family a most rare present: an old tunic that had belonged to the Child Emperor.

It was a black silk tunic lined with extremely thin yellow silk. I still remember that it smelled of mothballs and some other indefinable, but noble, fragrance.

My mother carried that tunic home like a proud peacock. No doubt her delight resembled that of the neglected beauties hidden deep in the Forbidden City who clutched their photos with the Emperor. Each knew that what she possessed was an illusion; yet each was perfectly willing to fool herself to assuage some vanity and pride.

The imperial tunic was given to my oldest sister. Several times a year, on special occasions such as New Year's, it was taken out and "draped" over my sister's tiny frame for a few hours; then it was removed, carefully folded, and returned to the heavy family trunk.

Time passed, and the tunic, at first so large on my oldest sister, became smaller and smaller until she could no longer wear it; then it was passed on to the second daughter, and so on down the line. You might say the tunic was taken out to be aired on our backs a few times a year. Finally it was my turn. I was number seven in the line of recipients. It was on Tet, New Year's Day, when, with great solemnity, my mother told me to push my hands and arms through the tunic's sleeves. But, alas, the tunic had become so worn and fragile it disintegrated in our hands and there was not much left to return to the coffer.

I cried my heart out that New Year's Day. I cried all morning. I thought then that I was crying because my luck had run out on the day when it was my turn to wear the beautiful imperial tunic. Now I realize I was crying for my mother's illusion, nurtured over the years, that one day she would be generously repaid for all her pains.

That same year the young monarch returned home to his throne, but instead of dipping into the imperial coffers to repay her debts as she'd promised, the Empress Dowager disappeared. Word got around that she was forbidden to see any of those who had helped her out while her son was away.

At the celebration after the birth of the eleventh child in my family, someone presented my mother with a bolt of gorgeous pastel rose satin. Before we knew it, my mother was announcing that sisters six, seven, eight, and nine would each receive a new tunic made from the bolt of satin. We could scarcely wait for the next important occasion in order to be allowed to wear those luxurious, shiny garments that were so cool to the touch. Then, my paternal grandfather decided to pass away. I saw my parents cry, and my brothers and sisters cry, so I cried too. In reality I was crying for those pink satin tunics that we were never going to wear. For there was a "great mourning" in the family, and my mother went and had those four new tunics dyed. As it turned out, someone botched the job, and the tunics turned out to be neither green nor blue. My father called the hue "autumn-withered cabbage pickle." Imagine a cubist painting as clothing. Patches and streaks of all shades were piled pell-mell. Still, we all said that we loved them, just to please our mother.

Gamely, we bore the pain of the awful tunics, and they did their best to withstand our brutality. We wore them and we rolled on the ground. We crushed them into balls and tossed them around. By the time they were truly worn out, the period of mourning had ended.

Once more, a friend of my mother's sent from Saigon a few yards of pink satin. Thinking the color too bright and immodest for a lady of her station, my mother once again had tunics made for the four of us. The new tunics turned out to be both too long and too wide, and, as soon as they were delivered by the seamstress, were put away for an auspicious day when we would be allowed to try them out. Occasionally, I would sneak into the room where the big coffer stood and open the lid. I would fish out a tunic and press it against my cheek. It would feel cool and smooth against my face. Sometimes I would drape it over my small body and sniff the faint odor of mothballs with delight. That "auspicious" day never arrived, however, when we could officially wear our pink tunics, for then one of my uncles died. Although this time we did not have to pass through a "great mourning," my mother still decreed that we had to be *in* mourning. So once again we wept for the beautiful tunics that had to be dyed—what else?—to cabbage-pickle hues.

By this time, my father had advanced considerably up the career ladder, so my mother abandoned her antique business. She also stopped taking photographs of the court ladies and doctoring them up. Perhaps to teach us that frugality was still important in our new affluence, each of us received a clay piggy bank. However, each year for the next few, our little pigs were methodically slaughtered in the name of contributions for the boys' school clothes. Of course, we girls understood when it came to the needs of the family and took it in stride. My mother was so pleased by our generosity that she promised us we could have our brothers' tunics when they outgrew them.

Years passed. By the time those second rose tunics, which had been dyed upon Uncle's death, had been worn to nothing, we were entering puberty. Although we had already reached the age of blushing, we had for street clothes our brothers' tunics which were made of stiff, black cotton. We begged our mother in unison to buy us new, really nice tunics. But she said, "Look here, girls! We still have plenty of tunics from your brothers. They're strong and durable. Besides, don't you realize that what you're demanding is expensive? When I was your age, all I had was a cotton tunic. And look at all the gorgeous things you kids have had. Remember His Majesty's tunic, and those rose satin ones . . . ?"

"Which," I added to prod my mother's memory, "were dyed the color of autumn pickles."

"Autumn, winter, whatever, but never mind about that."

My youngest sister chimed in. "But Mother, the last time we had anything made was four years ago!"

"My, my," my mother said, "you know nothing about frugality and economy. I can see that! When I was your age I had only one tunic, and a cotton one at that. And that's why this family is so well off today."

Sister number nine piped up, "Yes, we know all that, Mother. But you were the daughter of a district chief, and your father wasn't alive, while we are daughters of a province chief. . . ."

"Ladies!" my mother said. "Remember who you are talking to and mind your manners!"

"Ohhh," we wailed. "You don't care a thing about us. You only love our biggest sister, Hong. Now that she's married and gone you can't even eat or sleep because you miss her. Whenever she comes home and asks you for money, right away you go and take our little pigs and you . . ."

"All right, all right. That's enough for now. You'll get your new clothes."

Our mother didn't like that we complained about the unequal treatment we received. Our married sister, Hong, came once a month and each time there was a big brouhaha. Her visits turned the household topsy-turvy. Just to see to her needs drove everyone to distraction. On the one hand, she was a spendthrift and tipped the servants royally. And she treated us to unforgettable feasts. Often she would call in one of those traveling food sellers who would serve us delicious pastries right on our front steps. The only thing we held against her was her nasty habit of breaking our bamboo savings boxes. Once she discovered that we were keeping them for our dowries (that's what Mother told her) she plundered them at each visit. She rationalized this by telling us that we were investing in her tailoring shop, with, of course, our mother's blessing. But when she got married and sold the shop, we didn't get any of our "investment" back and we decided that our sister had been in the red all along.

But to return to the subject of the new tunics. At last our mother kept her word. Somehow she managed to extricate a bolt of pale yellow silk from the bottom of the old trunk and summoned a soldier who had been a tailor in my father's service. "Be sure to cut them extra big," she ordered him. "Leave lots of room, you hear. We like them cool and comfortable." We were already grown girls and we cordially detested roomy tunics that made us look as if we were swimming upright in them. "Cut them long, too, will you?" my mother said. But behind Mother's back we signaled that we wanted the dresses tight.

Once the dresses were ready and we tried them on, we laughed and cried. They were long all right, so long they touched our heels. And they were also tight, so tight we looked like sausages. We couldn't even bend our elbows. So we had to cut open the sleeves and add pieces to the armpits. But we did wear those tunics; after all, they were much better than those faded and worn, black hand-me-downs from our brothers.

What followed our pale yellow silk "sausage dresses" were some more made from rationed materials. The war was on and fabric was parceled out by the authorities. Only the most tasteless prints were available. In these outrageous patterns we looked like curtains, or worse yet, walking sofas, walking cheap sofas. Yet we braved the situation and wore our gaudy tunics with no visible embarrassment.

Somehow or other, life finally became a little easier. My oldest sister was doing fine. Once in a while she would send us boxes of clothes she no longer wanted. I remember there were one or two practically brand-new tunics. Sister Number Six picked the red one and I settled for the blue. We wore them on special occasions, like when we went downtown, and we simply ignored our friends' comments like, "The colors clash," or that we looked like "beauty queens in a picture" or didn't we "notice the weather" and so on. We ignored them. Of course we had no choice.

It was just like my mother to let others take advantage of her while she and her children did without. Thinking back, perhaps she herself never really had a decent dress.

Later, when I began to lead my own life—not very successfully—I tried to skimp a bit here and there. I was living in Hong Kong then and at the end of each year I would send my mother enough silk brocade for ten dresses. I was counting on the worst: Out of those ten, she might give away, sell, or whatever, at most nine dresses, so there would be at least enough left for her to have one dress made for herself. I was happy thinking that.

Then one day I received a telegram telling me that my mother was critically ill. I flew home immediately, carrying enough brocade for ten new dresses. She died while I was there. I went through her clothes picking out something to bury her in but found no dress made from the silk brocade I had sent earlier.

I remembered what a friend had said to me once: "Face it, my dear. You've had it! No more dreams!"

She had said it, of course, out of love and friendship. I had failed miserably at marriage and only returned from abroad in time to see my mother dying. Two failures! But didn't she understand I could still dream?

After my mother was buried next to my father, I returned to Hong Kong. By this time, I had all the money I wanted for fancy clothes, but the excitement was gone. I couldn't recapture those delirious emotions I had felt as a child of twelve when I crept into my mother's room and opened the huge trunk to caress those pink satin tunics that were ours and waiting for us.

I remembered what my father had said after our grandfather had died. "When children are young they don't understand things; they think their parents are hard on them, saying they can't do this and have that. It's not until they grow up and have families of their own that they understand their parents and really love them. And then when they want to show their gratitude, their parents have already passed away."

My father repeated that over and over and each time he said it, he couldn't hold back his tears.

I am now a middle-aged woman. In the process of growing older I have acquired a funny habit. Whenever I am in town and see beautiful fabric, yards of gorgeous hues and costly designs, I can feel myself falling into a trance. I spend a fortune on silks and brocades, enough for ten dresses, only to awake after the spree and remember that my mother is no longer in this life.

Translated by Vo-Dinh Mai

Fired Gold

Nguyen Huy Thiep

MR. QUACH NGOC MINH from Tu Ly village in Da
Bac district town wrote me a letter: "I've read your short
story 'A Sharp Sword,' which tells of my ancestor Dang
Phu Lan. I didn't like the detail concerning his meeting
with Nguyen Du.* The character whom you describe as
the strange, pure young man at the inn 'with a soul as
clear as mountain water' seems pointless. The song 'The
Discordance of Talent and Fate,' which you attribute to
Nguyen Du, while clever, is not really that clever. Please
come up for a visit and I will let you examine several documents that will help you see things in a different light.
My daughter, Quach Thi Trinh, will prepare some fish
and starfruit consommé, which I'm sure you will enjoy. . . ."

Upon receiving this letter, I went up to visit Quach
Ngoc Minh and his family. The ancient documents he
possessed were truly original. I then returned to Hanoi
and wrote this story. As I wrote, I freely amended and re-

The original title of this story ("Vang Lua") alludes to a proverb: Fire
tests gold, suffering tests virtue *(Lua thu vàng, Gian nan thu dúc).*

*A high-ranking diplomat, Nguyen Du (1765–1820) became the fore-
most classical poet of Vietnam.

organized extraneous details and edited the documents so as to make them consistent with the telling of my story.

In 1802, Nguyen Phuc Anh invaded Thang Long and, taking the royal name Gia Long, seized the throne. The new king was assisted by a handful of European advisors including, due to the recommendation of Bishop Pigneau de Behaine, the Frenchman François Poirée. The King called him Phang.

Ever since childhood, Phang had liked to wander about. He participated in the revolution of 1789 and was friends with Saint Just. In 1797, he boarded a merchant ship bound for Hoi An. While no one actually knows if a meeting between Phang and Pigneau de Behaine took place, the bishop definitely did write Phang a letter of introduction to King Gia Long.

In his diary, Phang writes,

The King is one colossal solitary mass. He performs his role in the imperial court with great skill. He moves, stands, exits, enters, issues orders, and receives homage from his clique of court officials. He is a stern father toward his selfish and dimwitted children. As a husband, he commands respect from his mediocre wives. He knows he is old, and with the young, beautiful concubines in his royal harem, he is impotent. As its founder and architect, he knows that the imperial court is superficial, and that his nation is poor. He worries constantly because he is aware that the power that lies exclusively in his hands is far too great for the strength of a single human being. . . .

Phang follows Gia Long on a hunting trip north of Hue, the royal capital. According to Phang:

> The King rides a horse, his back erect. In the wild, he is radiant, and the anxious scowl he wears daily disappears. He is happy, thrilled by the hunt. Sitting with me that evening he says, "Do you see that pack of dogs over there? They prepare everything for me. As I pass through the hunting grounds, they actually release the prey for me." Surprised, I ask why the King (by birth a skilled martial leader) tolerates this insult. He laughs: "You understand nothing. Is there any glory not attained at the expense of a good name?" Sitting there listening to the King, I am struck by the dreadfulness of his life. He understands that his existence is essentially dependent on symbiosis. As fate has arbitrarily placed him in a paramount position, he dares not tamper with any of society's fixed relationships, since this might upset this delicate symbiosis and weaken his throne. I ask the King about Eastern philosophers but he shows no interest. He responds, "They are all embittered by life. They are the past. Our concern is the present." Here, the King is visibly more engrossed in finishing his tiger ribs than in continuing the conversation with me. . . .

Phang gets Gia Long's permission to travel around the realm. He meets Nguyen Du, who at that time is serving as a district chief. Phang writes:

> Before me is a slight, young man whose face is creased with misery. This man is a famous and talented poet. I

sense that he understands absolutely nothing about politics, and yet he is an unswervingly dedicated official. His character is superior to that of others, yet what value does such character hold when real, material life is impoverished and luckless. He lacks even the most basic conveniences. He can be neither frivolous nor magnanimous. Spiritual life suffocates him. His speech is simple and cunning; his intuition, wonderful. Like Gia Long, he is also a massive bulk of material, but lighter, less substantial, and thus besmeared with thinner layers of soot and impurities. Both men are priceless treasures, national entities.

Nguyen Du takes Phang to visit several areas under his jurisdiction. Phang writes:

Nguyen Du displays a deep sympathy for the people. He loves his people and is himself representative of their most lyric and melancholic characteristics, but also of their most pitiable ones. Gia Long is representative of no one other than himself. Herein lies his glory, but also something horribly vile. The King perceives reality exclusively in relation to the perpetuation of his own existence. The King is aware of his own pain. But Nguyen Du is numb to his pain. Nguyen Du sympathizes with the odd miseries of small and isolated destinies but does not understand the general wave of misery welling up in the nation. The most significant characteristics of the country are its smallness and weakness. It is like a virgin girl raped by Chinese civilization. The girl concurrently enjoys, despises, and is humiliated by the rape. Gia

Long understands this and herein lies the bitterest sentiment that he and his community must endure. Nguyen Du does not understand this. Nguyen Du is the child of this virgin girl, and the blood that flows through his veins is laced with allusions to the brutal man who raped his mother. Whereas Nguyen Du appears to be drowning in the soft mulch of life, Gia Long stands tall, unencumbered, almost detached from that life. Nguyen Du's mother (the polity of that time) has, through supreme restraint and self-control, concealed her own shame and anguish from her child. Only in another three hundred years will we understand this seemingly meaningless gesture.

Nguyen Du lives a simple, country life and naively endures poverty with the people. He stands beside them and possesses no more than they do, which shows he understands nothing about politics. Because his days are filled with unproductive activities, he can only satisfy life's minimum requirements. His kindness is consequently of the small variety and is incapable of saving anyone. Gia Long is different. He himself is terrified by his own audacity in resisting the flow of nature and in deceptively using his people to serve his own interests. He certainly makes history more exciting. His is the immense kindness of a politician. This type of kindness is concerned not only with good works for their own sake, but with their contribution to the King's own force within the community. According to natural laws, each element in the community will exist, adjust, and develop. If one strong force does not exist, the community will stagnate and decay. The Vietnamese community suffers from an inferiority complex. How small it is next to Chinese civilization, a civilization equally glorious, vile, and ruthless. . . .

Phang describes Gia Long's impression upon meeting Nguyen Du:

The King listens to me disinterestedly. It seems he is deaf, but I know otherwise. He does not acknowledge Nguyen Du, or perhaps he simply considers him as one well-bred horse among many in the herds of horses, pigs, cows, and chickens that he must tend. "I already know this man," he informs us. "His father is Nguyen Nghiem. His older brother is Nguyen Khanh." I see that the King realizes Nguyen Du's helplessness in the face of his impoverished life and stagnant nation. He does not believe that the scholarly arts can transform his race. Priority must be given to the material situation. Unproductive economic activities offer the people only a meager and insecure existence. The problem at hand is how to rise up and strengthen the country. This will require the courage to withstand a swift and disorienting jolt to the community's fundamental structure of relationships. Decrepit Confucian practices and political masturbation will never result in pure or wholesome relations. A time will come when the worldwide polity will seem like an exotic mixed salad, and the very concept of moral purity will possess no significance.

In 1814, gold is discovered. Phang entreats Gia Long to give him permission to lead a band of Europeans on a search for gold. The King agrees. While Phang left no account of the expedition, an anonymous Portuguese participant did leave a memoir. According to the memoir:

Our band includes eleven men, four Portuguese, one Dutchman, five Frenchmen, and a Vietnamese guide. François Poirée leads us. Gia Long chooses to rely on this cruel man. We travel on horseback, carrying weapons and the kind of panning equipment used last century in North America. At this stage, François Poirée is unable to fathom the events that are about to unfold. For this, we ultimately pay a high price. Most of us have joined the expedition out of simple curiosity. We prepare enough provisions for one month. After snaking our way through the jungle, we arrive at a path. Here we find the source of a river peacefully lying within a deserted valley. No human shadow has previously passed over this place. A raven circles overhead. On his map, François Poirée names this place The Valley of the Ravens. We pitch tents along the river. That first day, the Dutchman suffers a convulsion. He progresses through several frightful seizures, his body grows hot like coal, his face turns gray. We suggest that someone remain behind to care for him, but François Poirée orders his dead body thrown into the river. A black swarm of ravens immediately descends upon the corpse. . . .

The gold mine is like a strip mine. We are overcome with elation and forget our exhaustion. On the third day, we are attacked by local natives. We cluster to-

gether in a defensive circle. Wielding knives and
spears from a safe distance, the natives hurl abuse
and shower us with stones. Their only intention is to
expel us from the valley. Seeing the attackers, our
Vietnamese guide disappears. François Poirée's Vietnamese is poor. He raises aloft King Gia Long's royal
banner, but to no effect. At that, we should hastily
withdraw, but François Poirée will not retreat. Instead
he opens fire. A native is hit. The rest run helter-
skelter. We implore François Poirée to let us turn
back, but he refuses to listen and forces us to return to
work. Dazzled by gold, he has become blind to reason. Returning that evening we see the skull of our
Vietnamese guide skewered on a stake posted near
our camp. Against a red-hot sky, a flock of ravens circle above the jungle, savagely shrieking as they fly.

In the middle of the night, a violent fire erupts
around our huts. Arrows soaked in deadly poison rain
down. Five members of our group are hit and die immediately. Seizing as much gold as possible, François
Poirée attempts to beat a bloody path of escape. The
fire grows unbearably hot. Before us, behind us, overhead, and underfoot, the entire jungle is engulfed in
flames. . . .

The memoir of the anonymous Portuguese ends here. I,
the writer of this short story, have already endeavored to
search the content of ancient texts and the memories of
aged men, yet I have uncovered neither documents nor
individuals with information on The Valley of the Ravens
and the Europeans who entered it during Gia Long's
reign. Over many years, all my attempts have been in

vain. I therefore offer three conclusions to the story, so that each reader can select the one that he or she feels is most suitable.

CONCLUSION ONE

Three members of the expedition survive, and Phang, with virtually the entire quantity of unearthed gold in tow, returns home. The expedition's success thrills the King. He orders an exploration The Valley of the Ravens and assigns Phang the task of overseeing the further exploitation of the mine. The two other surviving Europeans are also invited to participate, but they refuse. For two years Phang oversees the work in the mine. The King relies exclusively on Phang and bestows many generous awards on him. One day, the King sends Phang an elaborately prepared meal called Eight Jewel bird stew. After he eats it, a violent ache begins to gnaw at Phang's stomach. His eyes roll back in his head, blood pours from his mouth. He dies hunched over the dining table. Afterward, the following lines are discovered in his diary.

All human endeavor inspired by kindness is painful and exacting. Genuine kindness is as rare as gold, and ultimately it must be guaranteed with gold to have real value.

We live without meaning, poor and miserable among makeshift theories and specious reasoning, consumed with ethnic and class antagonisms. How fragile and trifling are our lives. When, I ask, when on the face of this earth, will progress appear?

CONCLUSION TWO

Only Phang escapes the sea of fire. With the remaining gold, he arrives at the house of the district chief. Showing the royal banner that bears the seal of Gia Long, Phang asks for protection. The district chief, an elderly Confucian scholar, is skilled in medicine. Phang undergoes treatment at this secluded district capital. Vu Thi, the young widowed daughter of the district chief, falls in love with Phang. When Phang returns to the capital, Gia Long bestows upon him a generous reward. The king orders the exploitation of the gold mine.

In Europe at that time, the monarchy of Napoleon Bonaparte lies in ruins. Europe matures. It begins to understand that the beauty and glory of a people are based on neither revolution nor war, on neither ideologists nor emperors. In grasping this, people can live more simply, reach their full potential, and be in greater accordance with nature. Phang requests Gia Long's permission to return with Vu Thi and a large store of gold to his native land. In France, he sets up a bank and lives happily for many years. With his grandchildren, he often conjures up stories about the historic upheavals he witnessed in distant Annam. According to Phang, the period during which he lived in Annam marked the beginning of the Vietnamese nation; borders were determined, a writing system based on the Latin alphabet became popularized, the Vietnamese gradually escaped from their frightful imprisonment under the Chinese, and a general intercourse was established with the community of humanity.

CONCLUSION THREE

All members of the gold expedition are killed. They were
in fact encircled and attacked not by the ethnic minority
peoples, as mistakenly reported in the memoir of the
anonymous Portuguese, but by dynastic troops. The
Europeans' possessions are searched for concealed gold,
their clothes and written records are examined. Gia Long
appoints a person of royal blood to oversee the exploitation of the mine. Toward the end of his life, Gia Long
lives in his palace, seeking to avoid contact with the outside world. The King hates anyone who dares remind
him of the early relations he had with Vietnamese,
Chinese, or Europeans back in the days when he was
poor and powerless.

The Nguyen Dynasty of King Gia Long was a horrific
dynasty. Please pay attention, dear readers, for this
dynasty has left many mausoleums.

Translated by Peter Zinoman

Scent of the Tiger

Quy The

"DARLING!"

I pretended to be asleep. I still wasn't speaking to her, and I refused to acknowledge her return, as usual, at midnight. I listened to her undressing, slowly removing her gold-threaded costume, hanging it on the hook by the door. I followed the sound of her footsteps into the bathroom. I heard light torrents of water splashing to the floor. Moments later, the creak of the bathroom door being gently pushed forward, I could feel her slide into bed next to me, softly pressing her body against mine. I sensed her completely, but was determined to remain aloof. We'd been fighting for over a week already.

"Why are you going to sleep so early?" she asked, moving her fingers lightly over my shoulders. I could feel her breath near my ear. "I have a surprise for you today," she whispered, wrapping her arms tightly around me.

Her body was wet and cool, while a very strange scent stirred me. It was the scent of rose perfume, a kind she had never used before. She felt so gentle, so soft in my arms, and especially alluring under the scent of roses. All of my senses were awakened by this scent, and in an odd way, I felt like I was with a new woman. And it seemed she also felt that way. Her gestures let me sense her happiness. Any resistance or anger I'd harbored melted away, effortlessly.

Our making up was that simple. While she was reasonable, never failing to make the first step, I always remained stubborn. Our silence toward each other had lasted the entire week, yet it had all started for a very simple reason. I had demanded she quit her job and she refused.

While I was a math professor at a well-known university, she, on the other hand, was a performer, a "tiger tamer" no less. In terms of fame, she was much more renowned than I, and her income was twice that of mine as well. Still, I could never get used to her "profession." It was too unconventional for me.

"I love tigers," she said. "They love me and I love my profession. What would I do if I quit this job? Be a secretary or a salesperson? It's not easy to find a new job. Moreover, finding an animal tamer like me is much more difficult than finding a secretary. Besides, I love the circus. Not only am I accustomed to it, but it's also a part of me."

Despite her words, I couldn't help but feel her job was very bizarre.

In fact, our entire marriage was bizarre. We had completely different professions and personalities. Before our wedding, people predicted we wouldn't last. But at that time we both ignored all the advice. I even found interesting her thoughts that our children would be as fearless as a tiger and as intelligent as I.

Our first meeting was, in a way, by chance. I was at the end-of-the-year awards ceremony at school, on the verge of drunkenness from several cups of booze my students had plied me with, when one student suggested we all go to the circus. Everyone agreed. The last time I had gone to the circus, I was nine. Since then, I had paid no attention to such kinds of entertainment.

When we arrived, the audience was applauding cheerfully, throwing flowers to a woman in a sparkling gold costume. Dazzling light from above illuminated her bright smile. At her feet lay three big tigers. I had never seen such an impressive spectacle: three Kings of the Jungle were submitting to this small woman! In a whirl of excitement, one of my students suddenly placed a bunch of red carnations in my arms. "Go over and offer these to the beautiful woman, Professor!" he said, pushing me toward her. Like a machine I found myself holding flowers up to a woman onstage for the first time in my life, and most of all, to a tiger-tamer. Looking up at her through my coke-bottle glasses, my face must have looked silly and out of place under the exciting Big Top.

"Perhaps this is your first time at our performance?" she asked me, smiling.

At a close distance, I realized she was very beautiful. Her face was graceful, her hair like burnished silk. I found it strange that her face was so bright and yet she wore no makeup. Maybe her beauty was a reflection from the glorious light of her success. In my profession, the world of academia, moments of such admiration by so many people are truly beyond hope. I said to her words that I had never said to any woman before: "I deeply admire your talent. After the performance, if you would agree, we could meet at . . ."

"Delighted," she replied in a deep, low voice.

Later we met each other often. We enjoyed each other's company, perhaps due to the unusual qualities of our relationship. According to her, ours was a unique combination of might and intellect. We finally decided to get married.

Our wedding was remarkable. My friends were all intellectuals, not prone to cracking jokes or smiling excessively. Her friends, on the other hand, were quite the opposite. They drank liquor, laughed loudly, and danced wildly.

I became fond of circus life that very day. First, the juggler grabbed four chopsticks and performed right at the party. Then the magician covered his soup bowl with a napkin, crying out: "Disappear!" Nothing actually happened, but he did provoke a burst of cheerful laughter. The clowns joked non-stop. Gradually the professors abandoned their serious looks and joined in the fun. In a moment of inspiration, one professor stood up and began to sing "The Beauty and the Beast"—just perhaps insinuating that I was the monster? Next to my beautiful wife, I was, I admit, homely.

"On your wedding night, Professor, watch out for the tiger's claw!" one acrobat warned loudly.

"Bride, remember to take the tiger-whip into the bedroom with you tonight. If 'it' acts out of line, lash it!" the horse rider yelled.

When night finally arrived, I was neither clawed nor lashed by any whip. The taller and braver she looked in the circus ring, the smaller and softer she felt in my arms. Before the wedding, I had never imagined she would be so gentle.

"An animal tamer must love and treat her subjects gently," she said that night. I was, perhaps, also an animal whom she loved and pampered.

The one thing that remained forever with me from that night was a strong gamey scent emanating from her body, especially from her hair. Later, I found out this was the smell of the tiger, an unforgettable scent.

After our honeymoon, years and years passed on; life was rather happy. We had very little time for one another. During the winter, she traveled with the circus. I also had engagements here and there, taking part in conferences, sometimes even going abroad. Because of our conflicting schedules, we valued the time when we were together. Usually, I had nothing interesting to share about my work. She, however, never failed to come up with some funny story.

One day, for instance, she told about Toto the Bear, who refused to go out into the ring. After much effort and confusion, the reason for Toto's stubbornness turned out to be very simple: it was Toto's day to begin winter hibernation. And then there was Dac Lac, a female tiger who was at least six feet long. Dac Lac was, according to my wife, the most charming animal, and she had just given birth to her first litter. There was also the touching story of an unfortunate goose that was stepped on by a horse during a performance. Before it died, the goose spread open its wings to embrace its trainer, whose tears were streaming down her face. She even swore that she would never tame another goose again.

I'm not sure whether my wife's coworkers teased her for marrying a professor. But as for me, my colleagues never stopped ribbing me. One young, beautiful, unmarried secretary at my college asked me if my wife forced me to jump through a ring of fire. Another woman, even more aggressive, asked me in a snappish tone if my female tiger clawed and howled in our bed at night. When we went out for walks, we often encountered people looking at us with curious eyes. I was annoyed by that, and after a while I stopped going out with her.

In general, my wife was very accepting of her unusual job and was never bothered by what others might think. On only one occasion did she seem to care. That was at the birthday party of one of my friends. The host's dog was friendly to everybody but her. It barked fiercely at her and even attempted to bite her. All the other ladies exchanged glances as if to say, "Look, they're fighting!" My wife felt uncomfortable and urged that we leave early.

"Do you also mind my scent, my tiger smell?" she asked when we got home. It was the first time she had mentioned that gamey smell by name.

Trying to reassure my wife, I gave her a soothing, although insincere answer, "No, definitely not. I love you and I also love your tiger smell."

"You lie, darling," she said, smiling. "I know you don't like it. Last month, you used our small bed as an excuse for us to sleep separately. Every woman should be sweet-smelling, but I, unfortunately, cannot."

"Why?" I quietly asked.

"Animals, especially tigers, recognize things through their noses, not their eyes," she sighed. "A strange smell means an enemy!" She dropped her eyes from mine and proceeded to speak in a low, sorrowful voice, "I know you're annoyed because I brought this animal smell into our bedroom."

And then, the night after we made up, she had an accident. When I arrived at the hospital, she had already died. Holding her small body in my arms, I cried in desperate pain. From her burnished and silky, dark hair, the scent of roses she wore the night before streamed into my nose. Under the bright lights of the hospital and in her circus costume full of blood, her face looked serene and tranquil, as if in a dream. I broke down. I had never wept as I did that day. "Why did you still do it when you knew what would happen more than anyone else? Is it because of my selfishness?" I almost screamed out, wishing to go to hell and be punished.

The next day, the circus master told me the whole story. He spoke mechanically, yet choked with emotion.

"Dac Lac had been sick for several days and became violent. Maybe because her husband had been moved to another female tiger's cage. I had a premonition of impending doom, so I asked your wife to drop out of the tiger performance. But she was firm. "No, definitely not. A tiger tamer cannot be a coward!" she said. Then she proudly entered the ring, to a round of applause. There tigers submitted completely to her whip. When it came time for Dac Lac to jump through the ring of fire, your wife stood in front of the tiger and snapped the whip in the air. Dac Lac jumped onto the high chair. Your wife then moved forward and raised the ring of fire. Suddenly I saw the animal crouching, staring at her in a strange way. I put my hand on the pistol under my shirt and flicked open the leather strap. Your wife sensed what would happen. She moved quickly, yet remained calm. She knew Dac Lac was about to attack her and that I would try to shoot the animal. 'Don't shoot!' she screamed. It was right then that Dac Lac fell on her like a huge rock. She collapsed. The cruel animal turned back. I fired and then rushed over to her. The white costume, glistening with gold thread, was now full of blood. The whole circus seemed frozen in terror. She then spoke her last words. 'Did Dac Lac die?' she asked in a weak voice. Seeing me nod, she closed her eyes sadly. 'Poor tiger, she still had four little cubs. It wasn't her fault. It was mine,' your wife lamented.

After that horrible minute, the band tried to play a broken military tune. We had to continue with the show, following circus tradition. But no one wanted to watch, no one wanted to perform anymore. The band finally stopped playing. The whole circus was silent as if in a tomb. Everybody waited for the news from the hospital. An hour later, hearing that your wife had died, I had to drag myself out into the ring to give the news. The audience refused to leave. So many flowers were placed at the spot where she had fallen. And the clowns lurched out, their eyes red with tears. . . ."

Translated by Nguyen Nguyet Cam and Jim Carlson
(with special help from Patricia Brown)

The White Horse

Nguyen Ba Trac

TO A COUNTRY as law-abiding and orderly as America, Mr. Nguyen is not a good citizen. When it comes to income taxes, he's a mess. He doesn't file his taxes on time. He spends everything he earns, while his salary comes to him without deductions. He is enthusiastic about sending gifts to Vietnam, but when tax filing deadlines arrive, he'll be penniless. This has gone on for three years.

To the bank, Mr. Nguyen isn't a favored customer. Like an American consumer, he keeps an account and checkbook, but does no accounting, even simple addition or subtraction. He is routinely fined for overdrawing on his account. His name is registered in books and kept in computers that can expose those with bad credit. People whose names are in these computers can't be trusted. There's no lending to such people. No mortgages for them. The banks send him polite letters apologizing for not wanting him as a customer.

To the Department of Motor Vehicles and the police, Mr. Nguyen is a careless man. In a span of three years, he has received over forty tickets for moving violations. His license has been revoked twice. In the computer, late charges on such tickets continue to multiply twice, three times the original amounts, becoming figures too large for Mr. Nguyen to deal with. The same violations keep recurring: running a red light, or a stop sign. Traveling too fast or too slow on the highways.

Why is he such a mess?

To be fair, Mr. Nguyen isn't exactly someone with an anti-social attitude. He's never been indicted. He's in relatively good health. He can't really complain about his mental health. When something fun happens, he can be jovial. He knows when he's sad. Nothing extraordinary about that. If he were to feel no pain, or not get burnt when he sticks his hand in a fire, well then that would be a surprise. But for a Vietnamese cast far from his family, his friends, and his homeland, mired in endless worries, remembrance, and sorrow . . . a mind churning with events, questions, introspection . . . in the final analysis, this is nothing extraordinary.

Morning: brushes his teeth, cleans his mouth. Goes to work. Eats his lunch. An evening meal. Sleeps when night comes. Runs errands on weekends: buys the odd pieces of black fabric, some tablets, waiting until he can fill up a gift box to send home to his family, parents, brothers and sisters, wife and kids. It's not a heavy schedule, but he's always busy. Why?

You can't say Mr. Nguyen lives in one place. Rather, he lives in two worlds: his soul is in America, but his spirit shuttles back and forth between America and his homeland way on the other side of the globe. One moment he's sitting beneath fluorescent lights, working among various machines, the next he's walking down a Saigon alley, beneath the shade of a fishroe tree. In addition, Mr. Nguyen lives in two time periods: the present and the past. He moves back and forth within his past. Sometimes he goes all the way back to a classroom in a Hanoi temple, reciting his ABCs alongside friends afflicted by eye and skin diseases. The next moment he speeds forward to a university dorm room, where he coolly whistles as he combs his hair, getting ready for a stroll in downtown Saigon.

Such a jumbled sense of time and space can consume his entire day.

You have to admit, the earth was once a massive thing. To travel once around the globe was quite an achievement. To travel with one's tent from Hanoi to Hue for the mandarin examination took three long months. But, things change. Airplanes and spaceships have shrunk the earth. Satellite photos from outer space reduce the earth to the size of an orange. Fascism and feudal regimes have gone out of fashion. The conflict between capitalism and communism wouldn't mean much either if the earth were attacked by aliens from Venus.

But even if modern technology has reduced distances . . . and no matter how fast a thought can travel . . . nothing can quite help Mr. Nguyen (as he sits behind the wheel daydreaming about his old neighborhood in the Ban Co District) to stop his car in time for a red light in America.

Usually, he can't make it.

So, the speed of a thought is really still too slow. And space is still too large. And Mr. Nguyen still has police cars chasing him with sirens screaming full blast and

lights flashing, all because of ancient reasons: running a
red light. Not stopping at a stop sign. Traveling too fast or
too slow on the highways.

In America, heaven and earth are turning white.

The green mountains have changed to a silvery gray,
and snow dots their summits. Darkness comes swiftly
now. People are shopping and celebrating Christmas, but
Mr. Nguyen hasn't stopped traveling back and forth between the past and present, between this and the other
side of the globe.

The turmoil between time and space creates more
complications than the damn traffic citations or bank
credit.

In moments of solitude, people's memories burrow
back into the deepest parts of a land on the other side of
the globe where they were born, digging up the upheavals
in history, a history either meticulously recorded or carelessly written, a history that people can begin to question
only now.

Memory takes people back to the Highlands, the Mid-
lands, conjuring for them the haunting calls of the Lang
Son rooster, even if they've never been to Lang Son before. Such memories are ephemeral. They are like the
foggy image of a boat leaving the Thua Phu bank to float
up the River of Perfume in a moonlit night, going up-
stream toward Thien Mu Pagoda, or Quan Thanh. If you
were to dip your hands into the water, you might imagine
being able to grab hold of the costumes of the emperors
from the Nguyen Dynasty, who once brought warriors
from the West all the way back to Vietnam. Such memo-

ries allow you to imagine how you once meandered about on a summer night . . . to imagine you're back near the Hang Co train station, looking for that insect that is sadness, the cicada . . . or that time when you watched the Moroccan soldiers from the French Foreign Legion.

For Mr. Nguyen, memory and an analytical mind create such headaches. For, if memory and an analytical mind can transport him to moments of past happiness, they can also fill his heart with pain. Unfortunately, thinking about the sufferings of the past doesn't help the heart to avoid being hurt.

Memory is a horse on an ephemeral path, but you can't stop it. It goes where it wants to go. It goes all the way back to Dalat, galloping freely upon green hills in an afternoon in which the hues of sunshine are as light and thin as smoke and clouds. In such moments, all he wants is for Mrs. Nguyen to hold his hand and to go wandering with her under the sun. The horse will stretch its body to take him at great strides back to his old school. To visit his old friends. Or the graves of millions of people. To relatives North and South, people who have gone through untold seasons of separation. People in prison. People hugging their knees in re-education camps. Men, women, children who died at sea. Bombs, land mines, traps. Russian weapons, American weapons, Japanese weapons, Czech weapons. Mongolian horses. Chinese swords and machetes dating from all dynasties.

Mr. Nguyen sits at work, his hands under his chin, ignoring the ringing telephone. He looks out the window and notices the arrival of the tenth winter. His memory forces him to examine himself and all his loved ones.

Even acquaintances. All the people born where he was born during a season of floods, three years before millions of people died of famine. A country that for several millennia has not seen the end of suffering.

Memory and an analytical mind take him back to the time when the French had just arrived in Vietnam with battle ships, cannons, boots. Fortress walls falling under rockets. Vietnamese heroes calmly taking poison. His memory takes him back to Christmas seasons, when Catholics were persecuted and missionaries arrested and executed; to a time when the first Vietnamese Catholics were considered bridges for Europeans to take over and dominate Vietnam. History and politics become headaches that haunt the Vietnamese mind wherever it lives in the world.

It isn't right to have to deal with worries of a political nature during Christmas. All misunderstandings must end. Christmas must be a season of love and joy.

It is now Christmas.

Streets are decorated with lights and flowers. Miniature red and green light bulbs surround the windows. Each home has prepared a lovely pine tree, properly placed in the living room. Americans seriously welcome Christmas just like the Vietnamese abandon themselves to celebrate their Tet festival.

The weather is clear and crisp. Bells toll, sending Mr. Nguyen back twenty-five years, when girls in white lined up in church to sing "Silent Night."

Mr. Nguyen tenderly remembers his first love. The girl whose smile was bright as an apricot blossom and sweet as an orchid had given him some fabric on Christmas Eve so that he could have a shirt made. For a seventeen-year-old boy, it was an overwhelming feeling. The girl had included a photo of Saint Theresa in a wooden frame as part of the gift.

These days, his heart is too old. It has grown too arid to feel the romance and saintliness of twenty-five years ago.

Still, the horse in his memory gallops back to that Christmas, gingerly returning to him such details as when he came home to tell his mother about the gifts. His mother said, "Then you must buy her a gift in return." His mother undid the safety pin from her pocket and took out three bills of five *dong* and handed them to him. He circled the shops on his bicycle but could not think of a gift for her. What could he buy her? He settled on a pair of red velvet sandals. They were small for his feet, but were still a size and a half larger than hers.

That Christmas Eve, when the bells sang out, she wore a white *ao dai* tunic with the oversized sandals, and toyed with a white scarf in her hands. She and other girls, also in white *ao dai,* stood solemnly on a wooden platform outside the church, looked upward, and sent their voices soaring into the sky above the city.

He thought then that each and every soul was lined up just as solemnly, silent as could be, listening to the song that penetrated the darkness. Listening to the gentle, joyful, echoing voices that sounded like bells from far away, swaying in the realms of ancient times.

> *In a holy night far away, a holy night long ago*
> *She stood dream-like in a quiet space,*

A girl in a white dress and a white scarf,
A pure soul singing poetic innocence.

The girl in a white dress and a white scarf with a pure soul wasn't really a saint. She moved with her parents to another province and Mr. Nguyen never saw her again. But she remains a pure soul forever.

Mr. Nguyen possesses a murky understanding of the Catholic saints, except, perhaps, the saint Theresa, the one in the photo that the girl had given him in high school. His understanding of Catholicism is just as murky. Once in a while, he reads the Bible, but remembers only a romantic passage: "Witness the bird in the wild. Without planting a seed, my father has allowed it to be properly fed. Witness the lilacs in the fields. Without weaving threads, my father has allowed them to be dressed in lovely clothes that even Solomon couldn't have."

When he was a child living in Hanoi, Mr. Nguyen used to stand in front of the church, watching people selling pictures of far-away Italy. Back then, printing technology in Vietnam was still rudimentary. There were pictures of floating angels or beautiful shepherds, saints with golden halos, Gothic architecture that provoked saintly emotions. Such images today continue to bring him to church during the Christmas season.

Mr. Nguyen's memory, a white horse raising its head to travel through golden fields and green hills, returns him to the sound of ringing bells from years past. Such bells ring out every Christmas. To tell the truth, his memory should rest there. Where there is a girl in her white dress and oversized sandals. She stands with her friends, forever looking skyward to sing for a peaceful and compassionate humanity. Such songs are always beautiful. Even if you're Muslim, Buddhist, or Hindu, or even an alien from Mars visiting the earth, you would feel peaceful inside. Who does not want such peaceful moments?

And if you happen to be thinking about such peaceful moments, and happen to pay no attention to the stop sign, or the red light, or your account balance, then the whole business about your bad driving records, your bad credit . . . well, such a business is really a lovely quality, not something to be punished for.

Translated by Nguyen Qui Duc

Contributors

JOHN BALABAN (editor) served in Vietnam as a conscientious objector during, later returning to collect and translate its oral folk poetry in *Ca Dao Vietnam: Vietnamese Folk Poetry*. His own poetry has won several prizes, as well as two nominations for the National Book Award. His is the author of a celebrated Vietnam memoir, *Remembering Heaven's Face* and the editor/translator of *Spring Essence: The Poetry of Ho Xuan Huong*.

NGUYEN QUI DUC (editor, contributor, and translator) is the author of *Where The Ashes Are, The Odyssey of a Vietnamese Family*, and the translator of the novella *Behind The Red Mist* by Ho Anh Thai. His latest book, *The Time Tree, Poems by Huu Thinh*, was a finalist for the 2004 Translation Prize by the Northern California Book Reviewers Association. His essays and short stories have appeared in the *San Francisco Examiner, New York Times Magazine, Asian Wall Street Journal Weekly, San Jose Mercury News, Los Angeles Times, Boston Globe*, and in anthologies and journals such as *Under Western Eyes, Watermark, Zyzzyva, City Lights, Manoa, Salamander*, etc. Since November of 2000, he has been the host of KQED Public Radio's Pacific Time. He was awarded the Overseas Press Club's Citation of Excellence for his reports from Vietnam for NPR (1989) and fellowship for outstanding achievements from the Alexander Gerbode Foundation (2005).

NGUYEN HUY THIEP, born in Hanoi in 1950, spent much of his youth in the rural provinces of Vietnam, where his mother worked as an agricultural laborer. After graduating from the Teachers' College in 1970, during the American bombing campaign, he moved to a remote province where he taught history, wrote, and painted. By 1987 he began to be published in the major journals in Vietnam, and in 1988 more than twenty of his stories were published. *The General Retires and Other Stories* was published by Oxford University Press.

DUONG THU HUONG was born in 1947 in Hanoi. At twenty, she led a Communist Youth brigade sent to the front during the Vietnam War. When China attacked Vietnam in 1979, she became the first woman combatant reporting on the fighting from the front. She has written four novels, two of which, *Paradise of the Blind* and *Novel without a Name* (excerpted in this collection), have been published in the United States by Morrow.

PHAM THI HOAI studied Archival Science in Germany and returned to Vietnam to work at the Institute of History in Hanoi. She has translated numerous western books into Vietnamese. Her novel, *The Crystal Messenger*, has been translated into six languages (the English edition is due out in 1996 by Hyland House). "The Saigon Tailor Shop" was published in the Literary Press's *Best Short Stories of 1994* in Hanoi. Her stories and essays have appeared in numerous anthologies as well as *Grand Street*. She now lives in Berlin.

HO ANH THAI was born in 1960 in Nghe Tinh. A novelist and short-story writer best known for his novel *The Women on the Island* and his short-story collection *A Fragment of a Man*, he is a veteran of the fighting against China in 1979 and is currently a columnist for the foreign service magazine, *World Affairs Weekly*, in Hanoi. His books include *Men and Vehicles in the Moonlight, The Other Side of the Horizon, Winter Has Come,* and *Out of the Red Fog.* He has won the Writer's Association award for best novel written in a five-year period.

LE MINH KHUE was born in Thanh Hoa Province. She joined the People's Army at the age of fifteen and spent much of her youth on the Ho Chi Minh Trail, serving as a member of the Youth Volunteers Brigade. From 1969 to 1975 she was a reporter for *The Vanguard* and Giai Phong radio. A short-story writer and novelist, her works include *Ummer's Peak, Distant Stars, Conclusion, An Afternoon Away from the City,* and *A Girl in a Green Gown.* She won the Writers' Association National Award for the best short stories in 1987. She co-edited the anthology *The Other Side of Heaven,* published in the United States in 1995. She now lives in Hanoi, where she is an editor at the Writers' Association Publishing House.

DOAN QUOC SY was born in 1923 in Hanoi and was part of the exodus to the South following the 1954 partition of Vietnam. He is the author of dozens of novels and plays, as well as collections of short stories, essays, and criticism. He taught at the University of Saigon until 1976 when he was arrested and placed in a re-education camp. From 1976 to 1991, he spent more than ten years imprisoned. In 1995, he was allowed to emigrate to the United States.

BAO NINH was born in Hanoi in 1952. He served during the American war with the 27th Youth Brigade. His novel, *The Sorrow of War,* about a writer coming to grips with his memories of the war and his own ability to love, won the Writers' Association award for best novel in 1990. It has also been published in the United Kingdom and the United States. His stories have also been published in *Granta* and in the anthology *The Other Side of Heaven.*

ANDREW Q. LAM was born in Saigon in 1963 and came to the United States with his family in 1975. He is an associate editor at Pacific News Service in San Francisco, writing about the tragedies and comedies of Vietnamese-American life and the painful contradictions of exile and adjustment. He has won several awards for his essays and reporting, including the Thomas More Storke International Journalism Award. He is the co-editor of the anthology *Once upon a Dream: The Vietnamese-American Experience.*

THICH DUC THIEN was (until his recent retirement) a reporter for *Tien Phong* (*The Vanguard*). He is now a reclusive monk. "The Colonel" was published in *The Forty Very Best Short Stories of 1994.*

VU BAO, a veteran of both the French and American wars, was born in 1931 in Thai Binh Province, North Vietnam. His works include the short-story collections *To Be God, Our Tanks, Your Father Was a Woman,* and *The Eldest and the Youngest;* the novels *Getting Married* and *Time Doesn't Wait;* and the film scripts for *The Starlets, The 89th Minute, Birthday Celebration,* and *Late Tears.* He is the editor-in-chief of the Vietnam Cinema Committee and vice-chairman of the Writers' Association. He was awarded the Best Short Story Prize by the *Army Literature and Arts* magazine in 1988 and 1989 and received the Best Novel Prize for 1991 by the Hanoi Writers' Association.

LINH BAO, whose real name is Vo-Thi Dieu-Van, was born in 1926 in Hue. A writer of essays, novels, and short stories, she was awarded the National Prize for Literature in South Vietnam in 1962. She has lived in the United States since then and is now a resident of Los Angeles.

Quy The was born in Nhatrang in 1956. He graduated from Saigon Law School and worked as a lawyer until 1975 when he became a teacher. He has since returned to practicing law, and is now a member of the Khanh Hoa Assocation. His writing has appeared in numerous Vietnamese publications.

Nguyen Ba Trac came to the United States in the early 1970s after graduating from Vietnam's Institute of Public Administration. He is the author of two collections of essays, poems, and short stories, *Floating Blades of Grass,* and *Tales of a Refugee with Average Headaches.* He is the translator of *Tears before the Rain,* Larry Engelman's oral history of the last days of the Vietnam War.

Permissions

"A River's Mystery" from *You and I* (a collection of short stories published in 1995 by Hanoi Publishing House) by Bao Ninh. English translation © 1995 Tran Qui Phiet.

"The Color of Sorrow" by Nguyen Qui Duc reprinted by permission of the author. © 1995 Nguyen Qui Duc.

"Dark Wood and Shadows" by Andrew Q. Lam reprinted by permission of the author. © 1993 Andrew Q. Lam. Originally published in *Viet Nam Forum*, vol. 14 and *Transfer Magazine*, San Francisco.

"Remembrance of the Countryside" by Nguyen Huy Thiep reprinted by permission of the author. English translation © 1996 Dana Sachs and Nguyen Van Khang.

"The Colonel" by Thich Duc Thien reprinted by permission of the author. English translation © 1996 Nguyen Qui Duc.

"How Long until the End of Bitterness?" by Vu Bao reprinted by permission of the author. English translation © 1996 Nguyen Qui Duc.

"Dresses, Dresses" by Linh Bao reprinted by permission of the author. English translation © 1996 Vo-Dinh Mai.

"Fired Gold" by Nguyen Huy Thiep reprinted by permission of the author. English translation © 1993 Peter Zinoman. Originally published in *Viet Nam Forum*, vol. 14.

"Scent of the Tiger" from *The Moon Light* (a collection of award-winning short stories published in 1991 by the Writers' Association Publishing House, Hanoi and *Literature and Art* magazine) by Quy The reprinted by permission of the author. English translation © 1995 Nguyen Nguyet Cam and Jim Carlson.

"The White Horse" by Nguyen Ba Trac reprinted by permission of the author. English translation © 1995 Nguyen Qui Duc.